Edward Cline

Running Out My Guns

In the War of Ideas

A Collection of Advices

Patrick Henry Press

Library of Congress Cataloguing-in-Publication Data

Edward Cline (1946 -)
Running Out My Guns/Edward Cline

ISBN 978-1481810067

Cover Illustration: 18th century 36-pounder muzzle-loading naval gun

Patrick Henry Press
Williamsburg, VA

Table of Contents

Foreword

CULTURE

Foreword

"When the Crown runs out its entire array of legal guns against a man like Mr. Wilkes or a Pippin, the gun ports of liberty should snap open in answer, one after another, to reveal the primed barrels of Mr. Locke, Mr. Sidney, Mr. Harrington, and that whole potent armament of enlightenment. The order of fire should be commanded by a master gunner, such as Sir Charles Pratt – he has not had a last word on the matter of general warrants – and the vessel captained by Aristotle."

> —Dogmael Jones to Hugh Kenrick, *Sparrowhawk: Book III, Caxton*

I have always felt a pleasurable catharsis watching a fiery, cinematic sea fight or naval engagement, such as occurs in *Damn the Defiant, Captain Horatio Hornblower, R.N.*, and *Sink the Bismarck*, to name but three fine seafaring films. And for years I have been manning my own gun, linstock (or cigarette) in hand, touch hole cleaned and ready to receive the slow match, the barrel elevated to fire at the enemy vessel's mainmast. The adversary has usually been some enemy of freedom, or a particular instance of cultural corruption, or a tiresome episode of the irrational. Rarely have I had the chance to close the gun port and secure the gun for a respite, and sail contentedly on a placid ocean. The battle against tyranny and piracy these days goes on and on, allowing little opportunity to rest. A nemesis is always appearing on the horizon. There are bureaucratic corsairs, and Barbary pirates, and cultural freebooters. They have all deserved my most truculent and merciless broadsides.

This volume of "advices" represents a small fraction of my nonfiction efforts over the last twenty years, and focuses chiefly on what I have produced and seen published in one form or another since 2001. Most of these pieces appeared originally on Rule of Reason, the blog site of The Center for the Advancement of Capitalism, and later on, on The Dougout and Family Security Matters. They have been picked up by or linked to numerous other Internet venues, here and abroad. They are exercises in comprehension, stages of anger, and *etudes* in identification. It has been a thankless job with very little in the way of prize money. But it is a necessary task, if freedom is to be preserved or recovered.

Edward Cline
Williamsburg, Virginia
December 2011

Campaign Button of the Bull Moose Party

Politics

A Miscellany of Sacred Cows

At the risk of offending Hindus and provoking further violent demonstrations against the freedom of speech, let us dwell for a moment on a few "sacred cows." In Western civilization, the term "sacred cow" disparages not only a person or thing unreasonably protected from criticism, but the Hindu belief that nasty-smelling, lice-ridden, parasitical, mooching bovines are holy creatures imbued with the privilege of deference because of their alleged association with a deity.

In the April 13th online English language edition of Pravda was an interesting article on the latest instance of the mental gymnastics that European Union officials are willing to demonstrate in their willingness to placate the hostiles, barbarians, and the Borg in their midst. It is to create a whole new herd of sacred cows, represented by a dictionary consisting of an "unemotional vocabulary used in conversations about radicalization." Read Islam. Defying the Aristotelian concept that A cannot be A and non-A at the same time, "Islamic terrorism" will now be called "terrorism which violently appeals to Islam," and "Islamic fundamentalism" will be "fundamentalism based on a false interpretation of Islam." Other proposed terms also dance around the fact that Islam means to conquer and exact submission by legal persecution, intimidation and force.

One cannot fail to see the pointlessness of the new wording. Aside from the fact that it is rooted in cowardice, it lacks economy in its homage to "sensitivity." But, Islam is Islam. Perhaps one could think of it as the difference between a waltz and a *minuet.*

On to other "sacred cows." Our host, Nick Provenzo, chastised Americans in his "Form 1040 and 'rational ignorance'" posting. He justifiably identified the fundamental culprit behind the byzantine Internal Revenue Code and the American penchant for submitting to it: altruism. But as I read it, two questions occurred to me: What is wrong with Mexico that so many people want to leave it? And, what is so attractive about the U.S. that so many Mexicans wish to come here? Why not to Venezuela, or Brazil, or Chile, all Latin countries in which Mexicans would surely feel more at home? And, they are also tax and regulation burdened welfare states. One has yet to hear a Congressman, Senator, or news anchor address these questions.

I recently received an amusing "letter" to the White House urging President Bush to persuade Mexican President Vicente Fox to grant Americans similar privileges and opportunities in Mexico as Mexicans enjoy in the U.S.: free medical services, the observance of the 4th of July, English-speaking teachers, police and bureaucrats, passport-less access to Mexico, class credit for American kids if they skip school (which would teach American history and culture) to demonstrate against Mexico, and other benefits.

If such a proposal were seriously considered, the outcry against American imperialism, racism, and other sins of commission would be immediate and loud. America is a "have" country, and Mexico a "have not," so it is America's moral duty to subsidize its own disintegration. So say La Raza and other nationalist "Latino" organizations, which hope to keep most Mexicans, legal or illegal, as clueless and semi-literate as American kids attending our public schools. Homogeneity and assimilation in the dominant or "host" culture is no more on their agenda than it is on the Islamist. Islamist groups joined Latinos in the recent demonstrations over the immigration uproar. They are allies now, but what will happen when they no longer agree to "divvy up" the U.S.?

But, Mr. Provenzo's comments also caused me to observe that a government that penalizes its citizens for not paying "their fair share" of taxes to pay off a growing debt that can never be paid, and, in fact, mandates the voluntary reporting of all income, whether in profits, salaries, wages, or even tips or gratuities, under penalty of prison and/or financial ruin, is not going to protect their freedom of speech.

Congress has not passed a law that compels citizens to file income tax returns, but rather has danced around that issue by arming the IRS with enforcement powers, powers that are not much different from those of the KGB or other political police apparatuses. If the government does not respect a citizen's right to his property, the issue of his freedom of speech must appear to any politician or bureaucrat as a niggling matter not worth exploring. Taxes are a sacred cow.

Or perhaps the subject is a powder keg.

After all, if the government championed the right of journalists and cartoonists to caricature Mohammed, it must necessarily and logically move to championing the right to one's property. The communication of a disparaging cartoon must employ the vehicle of property. But, to the government – local, state, or federal – private property is not sacrosanct. The right is not "inviolable." And so one can understand why the government would not want "to go there." To protect one right, one must eventually acknowledge other rights and act to protect them. To paraphrase Mr. Provenzo, Objectivism skewers that dichotomy rather quickly.

When reading any editorial, or listening to any politician such as the Treasury Secretary on the subject of taxes, one always reads or hears the phrase "your taxes," not "our taxes." Even H&R Block and Hewitt repeat it often, and apparently it has sunk into the psyche of the average productive American. The one phrase implies a moral obligation, the other an imposition. What a trick of semantics! The onus of responsibility, not to mention culpability, is put on the payer, not on the extortionist.

April, 2006

3

The IPCC's Square Pegs and Round Holes (or, Hockey Sticks)

The mushrooming Intergovernmental Panel on Climate Change (IPCC)-University of East Anglia-Climate Research Unit email scandal, dubbed "ClimateGate," invites satire first, then serious examination. We begin with an excerpt from the *IPCC Fourth Assessment Report: Climate Change 2007.* Read it and weep. There have been three other assessments, in 1990, 1995, and 2001. A fifth assessment is being prepared for 2014. What sold the IPCC on the credibility of global warming was the "hockey stick" graph of Al Gore notoriety. The fifth assessment – if it is ever collated and written – doubtless will feature baseball bats, the better to knock some sense into a doubting and skeptical public.

"The Fourth Working Group I Summary for Policymakers (SPM) was published on February 2, 2007 and revised on February 5, 2007.

The key conclusions of the SPM were that:

➤ Warming of the climate system is unequivocal.
➤ Most of the observed increase in globally averaged temperatures since the mid-20th century is very　　　likely due to the observed increase in anthropogenic (human) greenhouse gas concentrations.
➤ Anthropogenic warming and sea level rise would continue for centuries due to the timescales associated with climate processes and feedbacks, even if greenhouse gas concentrations were to be stabilized, although the likely amount of temperature and sea level rise varies greatly depending on the fossil intensity of human activity during the next century (pages 13 and 18).
➤ The probability that this is caused by natural climatic processes alone is less than 5%.
➤ World temperatures could rise by between 1.1 and 6.4 °C (2.0 and 11.5 °F) during the 21st century (table 3) and that:
➤ Sea levels will probably rise by 18 to 59 cm (7.08 to 23.22 in) [table 3].
➤ There is a confidence level >90% that there will be more frequent warm spells, heat waves and heavy rainfall.
➤ There is a confidence level >66% that there will be an increase in droughts, tropical cyclones and extreme high tides.
➤ Both past and future anthropogenic carbon dioxide emissions will continue to contribute to warming and sea level rise for more than a millennium.
➤ Global atmospheric concentrations of carbon dioxide, methane, and nitrous oxide have increased markedly as a result of human activities

4

since 1750 and now far exceed pre-industrial values over the past 650,000 years."

The IPCC was established in 1988 by the World Meteorological Organization (WMO) and the United Nations Environment Program (UNEP), both U.N. organizations. The 2007 Nobel Peace Prize was awarded to the IPCC and former vice president Al Gore. Well, we all know what the Nobel Peace Prize is worth. Ask President Barack Obama, this year's recipient.

The 2007 IPCC report contains and incorporates data cooked up by the University of East Anglia Climate Research Unit (CRU), headed by Phil Jones. The CRU bills itself as "widely recognized as one of the world's leading institutions concerned with the study of natural and anthropogenic climate change."

As one may see in the IPCC report above, not much global warming or climate change is attributed to natural causes. Less than five percent. The rest of it, according to the report, is all man's doing. Our activities are warping those natural causes. The qualifier in the report, "natural climatic processes," presumably exempts the sun from causing or contributing to those processes, provided one concedes that the processes are authentic and have happened or will happen.

The only value of any past and future IPCC report, to judge by the unearthed emails, is sensational material for doom-and-gloom science fiction movie producers, who would keep employed many special-effects graphic artists. However, the best source of news about ClimateGate is Climate Depot. Not the mainstream media, which, with Congress and the White House, is doing its best to ignore the scandal. After all, billions and billions of dollars are at stake if the cap-and-trade bill is not passed and if the Copenhagen climate change treaty implodes on its authors. Al Gore and his venal ilk stand to not profit if that happens.

Environmentalists, global warming advocates, and the government all have a vested interest in the "truth" of catastrophic climate change. Not to mention car manufacturers and other industries that have either retrofitted their plants or invested in "green" industries to comply with anticipated federal carbon legislation. Think of the billions spent on hybrid cars and florescent light bulbs and solar panels and wind turbines, all contrived to combat non-existent global warming. Poof! It will all have been for naught. So, the economic and political consequences of ClimateGate go far, far beyond the issue of the veracity of a handful of climate scientists.

The National Oceanic and Atmospheric Administration, a division of the National Weather Service, is stammering astonishment that CO_2 levels are not only not rising, but have nothing to do with global warming, which is not occurring. In fact, CO2 levels rise *after* temperature increases. The New York Times is "shocked, shocked" that fraud is taking place in climate science.

The New York Post ran an article on how school children are being indoctrinated (shall we say, "brainwashed") about the "reality" of global warming. Asked about ClimateGate, White House "climate advisor" Carol Browner pretended that she had never heard the one about fifty million Frenchmen being as wrong as one.

"What am I going to do?" asked Browner. "Side with the couple of naysayers out there, or the 2,500 scientists?" – who've drunk the Kool-Aid. "I'm sticking with the 2,500 scientists."

For a spot of sanity, listen to Lord Monckton, one of the original "skeptics" and "deniers."

The chairman of the IPCC, Rajendra Pachauri, has more or less said that the lies, frauds, and cover-ups will not affect his or the IPCC's conclusions about global warming.

Rajendra Pachauri defended the IPCC in the wake of apparent suggestions in emails between climate scientists at the University of East Anglia that they had prevented work they did not agree with from being included in the panel's fourth assessment report, which was published in 2007....The emails were made public this month after a hacker illegally obtained them from servers at the university....Pachauri said the large number of contributors and rigorous peer review mechanism adopted by the IPCC meant that any bias would be rapidly uncovered.

What he did not mention is that the "peer review" process was as rigged as were the data. Papers, findings, and statements by global warming "skeptics" and "deniers" were excoriated and deep-sixed as a matter of covert policy, apparently encouraged by CRU director Phil Jones.

Pachauri is concerned with neither the truth nor the lies.

Some commentators, including the former chancellor Nigel Lawson and the environmental campaigner and Guardian writer George Monbiot, have called on Jones to resign but Pachauri said he did not agree. He said an independent inquiry into the emails would achieve little, but there should be a criminal investigation into how the emails came to light.

Pachauri's first priority is to get the guy responsible for exposing the fraud and making him look like a fool. However, that "hacker" should be nominated for next year's Nobel Peace Prize. He has done the world a service that cannot be matched by any Prize winner in the past. He has uncovered the near pathological obsession of the IPCC and its acolytes with establishing a "world governance" body that would ensure that the world's population, and in particular that of the U.S., is reduced to the standard of living of men who lived in the Medieval Warm Period so neglected and blanked-out by the global warming harpies. That hacker properly invaded the "privacy" of men on government payrolls or who live off of looted taxes (e.g., Pachauri) who have advanced costly and elaborate junk science to attain a political agenda.

(One wishes that another hacker would raid the "private" emails of Nancy Pelosi, Harry Reid, Henry Waxman, and their health-care bill allies to see what *they* think of the trillion-dollar scam they wish to foist on this country.)

What is fascinating in a morbid sense is the almost hilarious evasive behavior of Phil Jones and his colleagues at the CRU as they try to fit square pegs into round holes. A Portuguese website, EcoTretas, contains many of the email exchanges between Jones and his co-conspirators as they scramble to counter the invasion of reality and truth-tellers. Many of the damning statements are highlighted by the site host. However, there are two un-highlighted statements that merit special scrutiny.

Under the heading, "Fixing the data," Jones, as long ago as 2000, complains:

> **From: Phil Jones, Date: Fri, 03 Mar 2000 13:04:24+0000**
> *As all our (Mike, Tom and CRU) all show that the first few centuries of the millennium were cooler than the 20th century, we will come in for some flak from the skeptics saying we're wrong because everyone knows it was warmer in the Medieval period.* **We can show why we believe we are correct with independent data from glacial advances and even slower responding proxies,** *however, what are the chances of putting together a group of a very few borehole [sic] series that are deep enough to get the last 1000 years. Basically trying to head off criticisms of the IPCC chapter, but good science in that we will be rewriting people's perceived wisdom about the course of temperature change over the past millennium.*

"*Everyone knows it was warmer in the Medieval period.*"So, let's forget it. Omit it from the picture altogether. More important is Jones's wish to "rewrite people's perceived wisdom." Which means: changing reality, or trying to. Which means: committing fraud and deceit.

Under the heading, "Wrongdoing," Jones, five years later, wishes again:

From: Phil Jones, Date: Tue Jul 5 15:15:55 2005
If anything, I would like to see the climate change happen, so the science could be proved right, regardless of the consequences. This isn't being political, **it is being selfish.**

But that damned climate just wouldn't change for the worse. The data just wouldn't conform to his wishes. How frustrating! It's more important to be proved right, than to adhere to and respect the truth that all indicators pointed to global cooling. So, let's just say that global warming is occurring anyway, that CO_2 is running amok, and that we're the cause, and it's getting hotter and hotter. Maybe nobody will notice. Repeat it often enough, and it will become true. Lots of friends in the MSM who will chant with us.

So the IPCC, Phil Jones, and his fellow Chicken Littles are all learning the hard way that square pegs have never gotten along with round holes. And that skies will not fall on command.

November 2009

Minds of Wax

*"Neither individuals nor nations become corrupt all at once,
nor are they enlightened in a moment."*

So observed William Wordsworth in 1815. He was commenting on the resistance to the revolution in poetry and in literature that was beginning to sweep through Europe as an overture to the Romantic Movement.

It would not be taxing credulity to observe, 192 years later, that neither the West nor the United States was corrupted all at once, or to wonder if the advocates of reason are fighting a rearguard action against the assaults on a retreating Western civilization, or are in the vanguard of reason, knowing too well in either instance that neither men nor nations can be enlightened in a moment. Chief elements of the corruption encouraging the assault are Kant's philosophy and the altruist/collectivist axis. When men abandon reason, whether gradually or immediately, a vacuum is created, and barbarism and irrationality rush in. This is what we are witnessing today, in virtually every realm of human life and action.

Reason seems to be impotent in the face of this multi-front onslaught. It certainly is not in the ascendant in current trends.

Dr. John Lewis of Ashland University, Ohio, was invited to George Mason University in Virginia, to give a talk, "No Substitute for Victory: The Defeat of Islamic Totalitarianism," and faced a form of this onslaught of anti-reason on the evening of April 24th. Although campus and local police were present, the barbarians established the anarchical tone of the event, continually interrupting Dr. Lewis with heckling and disruptive behavior.

At one point, the article reported, he replied to an uninvited comment, "The enemy is not Muslims. If you people [the "protestors"] refuse to hear this sentence, I can't help what's in your ears." ("No Substitute for Conflict," George Mason University *Broadside*, April 30)

Presumably, he meant wax, or rather the wax clogging their minds. Earwax, of course, can block hearing partially or completely, if not removed. And, it collects dirt, and can cause infection that can lead to a loss of hearing. "Wax" in the mind is immeasurably more harmful, and too many people today resist giving their minds a thorough scouring of the many forms of irrationality that comprise that wax.

Like people who hundreds of years ago believed that blood-letting was a cure-all for many kinds of illness, and resisted advances in medicine because they were "unnatural" or unsanctioned by God, many people today believe that closing one's mind to reason is a cure-all for most moral and philosophical conflicts. That is caused by the wax that accumulates in their minds by either faith or nihilism or Kantian "idealism" or emotion-driven subjectivism. Just as earwax mutes or blocks sound, these patently irrational methods of dealing with reality and other men mute the role of reason or block it entirely.

And what did Dr. Lewis say? Simply that totalitarian Iran is the U.S.'s biggest threat, that it seeks to impose its religious tyranny on as much of the world as it can, and that, like Nazi Germany and Imperial Japan, it must be defeated, militarily if necessary, if the West is to have any chance of survival.

This, the "protestors" did not wish to hear, nor wish anyone else to hear. Their minds were infected, of their own choice, at the behest of their religion or their professors. (Ayn Rand might have referred to it as "venomous muck.")

(I disagree with Dr. Lewis on only two points: Muslims are as much an "enemy" as devout Christians, environmentalists, left-wing student protestors, and power-seeking politicians; their minds are also closed to reason by choice or by mental lethargy. More on these phenomena below.

Elsewhere in the *Broadside* article, he is cited as believing that Islam is a "religion of peace," and that the problem with it is its application as a political ideology that denies a separation of church and state. But Islam is not a pacific creed; it is a supremacist creed whose fundamental tenets mandate its hegemony by force, guile or dissimulation in its means and ends.

I see no difference between Islam, Nazism, Shintoism and any other vile ideology that requires uncritical, unquestioning faith and the ready submission of its followers. It requires of men an internal comfort level with totalitarian ambience, and the granting by them to authoritarians or totalitarians an omniscience that relieves the believers of the task or responsibility of questioning party lines, dogmas and consensus-founded "truisms.")

Why is it so difficult to enlighten men? Reason is not so radical a means of resolving conflicts or answering questions. It has been an operative in Western culture since the Renaissance; if it had not been, no "West" would have come into existence. However, it has not been consistently applied to all human affairs; in some instances, not at all.

But, when reason is applied to a specific critical issue, what can account for the resistance to what it prescribes as proper actions to take? Why is reason rejected so hastily, or so volubly, so finally? In the GMU protestors' case, it is a matter of active resistance to it, prompted by malice or hostility to it as a resolution to problems or to the values reason seeks to advance or preserve; in many others, it is a matter of lethargic, passive

10

resistance, or a disinclination to think, or a preference to rely on undisputed, supposedly infallible authority, augmented by whatever irrational, fallacious ideas an individual has absorbed in the culture and never bothered to scrutinize.

At the risk of carrying the wax metaphor beyond bounds, a few instances might help to illustrate the malady.

At a recent booksigning for my *Sparrowhawk* novels outside the bookstore at Colonial Williamsburg where I appear every weekend, a prospective buyer asked me if I had written a book about the founding of Jamestown. Since I was having an informal conversation with the man and his party, I turned and pointed inside the store to a display of books on Jamestown by over a dozen authors, and exclaimed in a friendly manner, "Jesus Christ! I don't think they need *another* book about Jamestown! Everyone and his mother is writing about Jamestown!" Then the man's wife gave me an odd look and said to me, "You swore."

I learned later that the woman made a point of informing a store clerk that she had persuaded her husband not to buy a whole set of the series, as he had wanted to, because I "swore." There was a mind of wax in action. (Which is just as well, since they would have discovered that religious clerics do not fare well in the series; it was secular ideas of liberty that moved the American patriots, not religious ones.)

Moving to a broader issue, the *Daily Telegraph* (London) reported on April 30, under the headline, "Britain damaged by dropping arms deal inquiry," that Britain's Serious Fraud Office (SFO) was dropping an investigation of corruption connected with a multi-billion dollar arms deal with Saudi Arabia.

"The decision followed a Saudi threat to cancel a £10 billion order for new Typhoon fighters, a move which threatened thousands of jobs in the defense industry.

"Despite widespread criticism, Tony Blair defended the decision by arguing earlier this year that the SFO inquiry would have a 'devastating' impact on Britain's relations with Saudi Arabia if it was carried on."

Here is evidence of a great mound of wax. What possible benefit could Britain reap by maintaining "relations" with Saudi Arabia, except an arms deal that would prop up its subsidized arms industry? Why would it want to sell advanced fighter jets to a feudal monarchy that is using much of its oil revenues to stir up British Muslims and advance the Muslimization of Britain? If kickbacks, briberies, and other forms of corruption indeed characterize the arms deal, shouldn't the Saudi threat to cancel the deal imply their reality and indicate the Saudis' fear that corruption would be exposed?

Why are "good relations" with one's de facto enemies regarded as indispensable, but not the truth? But, these questions will not occur to Tony Blair or anyone else in his government, because the imperatives of unreason trump reason. The wax of pragmatic diplomacy is proof against reason. It will not penetrate.

Meanwhile, speaking of pragmatic diplomacy, on May 3rd, at a Middle East conference in Sharm El-Sheik, Egypt, Secretary of State Condoleezza Rice exhibited her own mind wax by stooping to meet with Walid Moallem, foreign minister of Syria, a state sponsor of terrorism and training ground for foreign "insurgents" it sends into neighboring Iraq to kill Americans and continue the unacknowledged civil war there. So much for President Bush sticking to his principle of never dealing even indirectly with Syria or Iran. The mind waxes of faith in God and faith in his goal of "democratizing" Iraq at the cost of American blood and treasure have for the last five years plugged up his receptivity to reason.

Does it matter to the Bush administration, or even to its Democratic opponents in Congress, that the U.S. military has evidence that Iran declared war on the U.S. by supplying Iraqi "insurgents" with ordnance with which to kill American soldiers? According to the *World Tribune* of May 1, this ordnance is not only of Iranian manufacture, but much of it is of Chinese origin, as well. Also, agents of Iran's Revolutionary Guard have been directing the "insurgency." No, none of this matters. Evidence is a product of reason, which is barred from playing a role in the formulation of foreign policy.

The "Goebbels" of global warming, Al Gore, has apparently instituted a "climate change" project which has trained over a thousand climate "messengers" to indoctrinate Americans in schools and businesses with the propaganda that man is responsible for melting icebergs, rising sea levels, and foul weather. Arguably the most culpable in helping Gore spread this propaganda is the news media, whose "reporters" and alleged journalists treat the fallacy as rock solid truth and who evince not the least inclination to question Gore's assertions.

Arguments offered by scientists who question Gore's assertions are either sidelined or not reported at all. The truth about global warming apparently is "inconvenient" enough to discourage the news media and most politicians from dislodging the wax of "consensus" from their minds. It is safer to repeat banalities.

What this culture needs is a firestorm of reason that will melt the wax that has been incrementally smothering this nation and the West for the last century.

Got a light?

May 2007

America vs. Congress et al.

If one wants to understand why Congress and the White House wish to sneak in "corporate" socialism in the guise of a "bailout" of Wall Street and the American economy, the following ought to serve as a good starting point, and provide some context of why the government thinks it ought to take action:

> "The accounts of the receipts and expenditures during the year ending on the 30th day of September last, being not yet made up, a correct statement will hereafter be transmitted from the Treasury. In the meantime, it is ascertained that the receipts have amounted to near eighteen millions of dollars, which, with the eight millions and a half in the treasury at the beginning of the year, have enabled us, after meeting the current demands and interest incurred, to pay two millions three hundred thousand dollars of the principal of our funded debt, and left us in the treasury, on that day, near fourteen millions of dollars….The probable accumulation of the surpluses of revenue beyond what can be applied to the payment of the public debt, whenever the safety and freedom of our commerce shall be restored, merits the consideration of Congress. Shall it lie unproductive in the public vaults? Shall the revenue be reduced? *Or shall it rather be appropriated to the improvements of roads, canals, rivers, education, and other great foundations of prosperity and union, under the powers which Congress may already possess, or such amendment of the constitution as may be approved of by the States?* While uncertain of the course of things, the time may be advantageously employed in obtaining the powers necessary for a system of improvement, should that be thought best." (*Italics* mine)*

So wrote President Thomas Jefferson in his last message to Congress in November, 1808. In past addresses and messages to Congress he reported revenue surpluses, and often recommended the reduction or abolition of taxes. The last time the federal government reported an actual surplus that did not reflect bookkeeping legerdemain and an appropriations shell game was during Calvin Coolidge's administration. In Jefferson's and Coolidge's instances the surpluses were in gold and silver currency and metal-based promissory notes, not in the baseless fiat paper and clad-zinc coinage of today. Gold and silver cannot be created by the snap of one's fingers or by an order from the Federal Reserve to cover deficits and debts, as fiat money is now. Gold and silver served as restraints on government spending and intervention, which is why FDR took the U.S. off the gold standard, and why silver coinage vanished by government order after 1965.

Without going into detail about past, pre-Federal Reserve Bank episodes of financial panics – such as the one Alexander Hamilton managed in 1792, the two Bank of the United States experiments, and the Panic of 1907 – it should be stressed that neither the participants nor the institutions involved sought to take over the entire American economy – that is, attempt to "socialize" or "nationalize" it – as the White House, Congress, the Federal Reserve Bank, and the U.S. Treasury are proposing to do now. It should also be pointed out that in none of those instances was the U.S. government the chief instigator or culprit, as it is today.

Another interesting facet of the government-made financial crisis is that two of the entities that needed to be "rescued" by the government, Fannie Mae and Freddie Mac, are government-founded mortgage companies created to sell and invest in cheap credit and cheap mortgages. There was no other purpose to their existence. They were created to "serve the public." Treasury chief Henry Paulson and Federal Reserve chief Bernard Bernanke have nothing over Scottish banker John Law, author of the Mississippi Bubble in early 18th century France. Their fiscal policies and economic philosophy are so similar to Law's that one would think Law was their mentor, but they have blanked out the ruinous consequences of the same schemes.

Nevertheless, Fannie Mae and Freddie Mac have been portrayed by Congress and the news media as independent of the government, when in fact they are taxpayer-subsidized. In a genuinely free market, an organization that behaved as recklessly as they did would have gone bankrupt and vanished from the scene. But because they were tax-subsidized, risk was no object, American taxpayers being seen by them and Congress as an inexhaustible cash cow. This was also the operating philosophy of Bear Stearns, Lehman Brothers, Merrill Lynch, and AIG, four of their biggest "customers." They are government entities that hire their own lobbyists to shill for special favors and treatment from – the government.

Financial skullduggery is not the only offense that Fannie Mae and Freddie Mac have committed. Their employees, whose salaries are paid by taxpayers, have also "invested" in the perpetuation of their jobs by sending money to the campaigns and pet pork barrels of Senators Barack Obama, Hillary and Bill Clinton, Christopher Dodd, chairman of the Senate Banking Committee, and many other politicians.

But both political parties, the Democrats and the Republicans, must share responsibility for the debacle. To wit:

"In 1971, Richard Nixon rescued Lockheed by providing $250 million in loan guarantees. When the Penn Central Railroad failed in 1971, Nixon created Amtrak. Jimmy Carter gave $1.5 billion loan guarantees to Chrysler in 1979. Under Ronald Reagan, the FDIC in 1984 spent $4.5 billion to rescue Continental Illinois, which still holds the record as the largest U.S. bank failure. Then, during the S&L crisis of the 1980's, George H.W. Bush approved the bailout of 747 savings and loans at a cost to taxpayers of $124.6 billion. In 1998, under Bill Clinton, the Federal Reserve Bank of New York bailed out Long Term Capital Management at a cost of $3.6 billion. During the Mexican Peso Crisis, Clinton arranged for loans and guarantees to Mexico totaling almost $50 billion. Then, following the September 11, 2001, terrorist attacks, George W. Bush approved $15 billion in subsidies and loan guarantees to aid the faltering airline industry. This year, the Federal Reserve approved a $30 billion credit line to help JP Morgan Chase acquire Bear Stearns, and engineered takeovers of Freddie Mac, Fannie Mae and AIG."

Topping all that is the $1.8 trillion the federal government will have shelled out to "save" the economy if Congress approves the proposed "bailout." All "guaranteed" by the American taxpayer. Only one senator has been reported as calling the Paulson/Bernanke/Bush/Pelosi/Frank plan "socialism," Jim Bunning of Kentucky. That was accidentally, and it is likely the news media will not let that kind of remark slip through the cracks again.

But, to return to the subject at hand, and to the italicized portion of Jefferson's message to Congress in 1808, the Founders could not imagine that "improvements of roads, canals, rivers, education, and other great foundations" could be financed by other than government intervention and government money. One may forgive Jefferson and his contemporaries for not being politically omniscient or infallible. Capitalism was in its infancy and the Industrial Revolution lay a generation ahead beyond his last administration. Not even the worst of his contemporaries could imagine that the premise of government responsibility for infrastructure and education could lead to anything but to the "prosperity and happiness" of the nation. There was nothing in the original Constitution that gave the government the power to "improve" the economy, either, except, implicitly, to let it alone.

Instead, that premise has repeatedly led to scandal, corruption, the destruction of wealth, and the looting of the productive sector – with the private, productive sector blamed and punished. It is time to begin challenging that premise, and get the government out of the economy, and especially out of education. Jefferson's benevolent but erroneous support of public education has ultimately, by necessity, over the course of generations, created a dumbed-down, docile public, one that expects the government to take care of it and solve all problems, real or imagined.

In my original commentary on this subject, I wrote that Congress, the White House, and the other "rescuers" were acting to stave off the pressure-cooked justice of the wrongdoing and fallacious policies of decades. Perhaps the only thing that will educate the American public now is the failure of the system which they were told, and which they believed, was justice-proof.

Then Americans may rise up, as the polls seem to show them doing now in demonstrations and calls to their Congressmen, to proclaim, "Account overdrawn!"

Thomas Jefferson: Writings, Library of America, 1984, pp. 548-549

September 2008

Portrait of a Police State

"Give me your tired, your poor,
Your huddled masses yearning to breathe free...."
Portion of Emma Lazarus's poem for the Statue of Liberty

The chief thrust of this article is that none of this would occur, or even be thought "necessary," if we had eliminated states that sponsor terrorism after 9/11. But when one reads the text of Senate Bill 1867, the National Defense Authorization Act (NDAA), one gets the impression that many in positions of power and influence, particularly Republican Senator John McCain of Arizona and Democrat Senator Carl Levin of Michigan, have a vested interest in sustaining an indefinite "war" against terrorism. This would entail establishing, or laying the groundwork for, a police state in which citizens would be lawfully accountable to the state, and not the other way around.

Fundamentally, they have a vested interest in waging a war against America and individual rights. Many sections of the bill are overtures to establish a permanent police state or an authoritarian government. As with many instances of legislation in the past, the bill is chiefly a finance bill, but contains riders, amendments, and sections that have little to do with finance but whose inclusion requires that their authors and sponsors resort to contemptible subterfuge.

One of the consequences of not having properly defended this country from attacks by our enemies – and Islam is certainly an enemy, the strenuous denials of George W. Bush and President Barack Obama to the contrary notwithstanding – is that to defend the country against "terrorism" without taking effective and final action against those enemies, the government must establish a "Fortress America," or policies which not so much ensure our protection as ensure the survival of the government. What happened to our liberties? They take a back seat. Eventually, they must be thrown from the vehicle of statism.

The Library of Congress inexplicably removed the links I found to the two versions of Senate Bill 1867 (my search was "timed out" and the links no longer work), but I found another one that contains the text of the bill. I have also included separate links to the texts of the notorious Sections 1031 and 1032, which discuss detention of U.S. citizens. These two sections were opposed by some Senators without success. Senators McCain and Levin sponsored the bill and were its principal architects, drafted in secret with not much to-do and only now making its debut. It almost makes one sigh with relief that McCain lost the 2008 election (Was the alternative any better?) The heading of Section 1031 reads:

Sec. 1031. Affirmation of authority of the Armed Forces of the United States to detain covered persons pursuant to the Authorization for Use of Military Force.

Despite assurances in the bill of Constitutional guarantees, the Secretary of Defense and the director of national intelligence may "waive" the inapplicability of Sections 1031 and 1032 to U.S. citizens after leave from Congress to do so. The assurances are merely devious lip service to a document that has been all but gutted of meaning, and to a political philosophy that began to expire with the Sherman Antitrust Act of 1890. (Some would argue that it began to expire with the first imposition of the draft and income tax under President Abraham Lincoln, but that's another story.) A paragraph of Section 1032 reads, in relation to the status of American citizens who may or may not be detained by the military:

32. (4) WAIVER FOR NATIONAL SECURITY.—The Secretary of Defense may, in consultation with the Secretary of State and the Director of National Intelligence, waive the requirement of paragraph (1) if the Secretary submits to Congress a certification in writing that such a waiver is in the national security interests of the United States.

From the McCain-Levin bill:

ACT OF TERRORISM- The term `act of terrorism' means an act of terrorism as that term is defined in section 101(15) of the Homeland Security Act of 2002 (6 U.S.C. 101(15)).

The term "terrorism" means any activity that - (A) involves an act that - (i) is dangerous to human life or potentially destructive of critical infrastructure or key resources; and (ii) is a violation of the criminal laws of the United States or of any State or other subdivision of the United States; and (B) appears to be intended - (i) to intimidate or coerce a civilian population; (ii) to influence the policy of a government by intimidation or coercion; or (iii) to affect the conduct of a government by mass destruction, assassination, or kidnapping. (16)(A)

The left is up in arms over the bill because Sections 1031 and 1032 do specify that captured or apprehended enemy combatants or agents who happen to be U.S. citizens or legal alien residents, and who have taken "hostile" actions against the U.S., may be detained without trial. The Left is more concerned with that than with the power of waiver granted to the government. Terrorists, apparently, have rights, but not their victims. But terrorists – the homegrown or foreign kind – have forfeited all rights by attacking the government and country that upholds individual rights with the purpose of destroying it and imposing totalitarian rule – whether that rule is Nazi, Communist, Fascist – or Islamic.

Lindsey Graham and other defenders of the bill's controversial riders referred to the United States as inclusive in a global "battlefield." On a battlefield, however, there are no rules of combat or engagement. One kills, wounds, or captures as many of the enemy as possible, with all means available. A battlefield is the stage of focused, controlled violence. Graham's remark was inappropriate, but reveals his estimate of his country and its citizens. His "battlefield" analogy is reminiscent of the propaganda of Nazi Germany, Communist Russia and Fascist Italy, where citizens were constantly reminded that the "battlefield" was their homes, their jobs, their families, their leisure, their churches, their friends, and the enemy anyone who opposed, resisted or questioned the respective ideology.

Not covered by either McCain's bill or the Homeland Security Act is the subject of *war*. What is an "act of war" but what is covered in the definition of "terrorism" cited above? Why has our attention been diverted from 'acts of war" to "acts of terrorism"?

(4) the term "act of war" means any act occurring in the course of —

(A) declared war;

(B) armed conflict, whether or not war has been declared, between two or more nations; or,

(C) armed conflict between military forces of any origin;

War would mean armed conflict with the advocates and enablers of another ideology. War means open, armed hostility, not necessarily for the enemy nation's cultural sum, but for its political ideology. A "war on terrorism," however, discards the ideology and focuses on the enablers (plotters, foot soldiers, etc.) as though they come from some generic template, and does not declare war on what motivates the plotters, soldiers, and so on. Neglecting to oppose and refute the enemy's ideology while focusing only on its carriers, propagators and advocates, is futile.

One could say that one cannot be at war with Islam, because Islam, as an ideology, seems to be "stateless." But, is it? No. Islam is what governs Saudi Arabia, Iran, Syria, Pakistan, Afghanistan, Egypt and all of the North African states. Islam is not some disembodied entity that infects individuals and causes them to fly planes into buildings or attempt to suppress freedom of speech. Islam is not the common cold. It isn't even typhus, or influenza. It is the bubonic plague of the mind.

If Islam declares war on freedom of speech, then it has declared war on an ideology, that is, on the political philosophy that professes and upholds the universality of individual rights. Why is it deemed inappropriate to declare war on Islam? Because it is also a theology? Because it propagates and perpetuates the belief in a supreme being or all-knowing and omnipotent deity? Christianity does that, as well, but Christian doctrine has been boxed in and stripped of the power to enforce its doctrine on all. One may believe in God or not; belief in a deity is immaterial in a society governed by secular law. There are those, of course, who assert that God is the source of all individual rights, but such a position ignores reality; it defies the law of identity and the evidence of the senses, as well.

Islam, however, cannot be boxed in or delimited in its political ambition. Its politics and theology are cut from the same cloth, which is belief without reservation, question, or doubt.

Ayn Rand posited a handy and eminently appropriate characterization of the dichotomy that can be applied to Islam: the *Witch Doctor* and *Attila*. The Witch Doctor depends on Attila to impose his mysticism; Attila depends on the Witch Doctor to sanction his reign of force. The Witch Doctor stands for the mystics of the mind – don't question, doubt, or think, just believe – while Attila is the mystic of muscle – force is the solution to all problems. The Witch Doctor is any imam or mullah or ayatollah or sheik; Mohammad is their ideal Attila. (While Allah, as portrayed by Islamic scholars, is the perfect symbol of the mystics of mind and muscle, a being governed by whims and who is not governed by reality or morality).

It is noteworthy that while the government, on one hand, is bowing to the complaints of Islamic activists (the Council on American-Islamic Relations and its Muslim Brotherhood affiliates) and is culling all references to Islam and Muslims from defense documents and training materials and courses for counter-terrorism, on the other, Senators McCain and Levin do mention Al-Quada and the Taliban in their bill (Section D, 1031). But Al-Quada and the Taliban are nothing if not Islamic organizations, from their burqa tops to the hems of their thawbs.

Put one way, the organizations charged with defending the country against terrorist attacks – the CIA, the FBI, and state and local law enforcement entities – are expected to conduct the "war on terrorism" blindfolded, dizzy from being turned around dozens of times by contradictory orders and criteria, and armed with a stick with which to strike at an empty piñata, which is moved away from them every time CAIR or some other Islamic front organization cries "victim" or "Islamophobia." *

> Representative Justin Amash (R-MI) wrote today on his Facebook page that S. 1867 is "one of the most anti-liberty pieces of legislation of our lifetime." Moreover, Amash maintains that the bill capitalizes on misleading semantics; regarding section 1032, he says "'The requirement to detain a person in military custody under this section does not extend to citizens of the United States.' This language appears carefully crafted to mislead the public. Note that it does not preclude U.S. citizens from being detained indefinitely, without charge or trial, it simply makes such detention discretionary."

But, who is defined as a U.S. citizen? And if a U.S. citizen wages war against his own country, should he not be charged with treason? And if he is charged with treason, is he not entitled to the full protection of the Constitution he wished to obviate?

Does the bill genuinely define a belligerent as an individual or "person," whether or not he is a U.S. citizen, who has taken up arms against the U.S., or has taken actions within its jurisdiction with the purpose of subverting or overthrowing the government or harming its citizens or "infrastructure"? Does it specifically exclude newspaper columnists, writers, satirists, or Internet bloggers, or anyone else who questions the wisdom or morality of government policies?

The six-hundred-plus pages of Senate bill 1867 do not answer these questions. This bill is the kind of legislation that is knocked together in the purgatory of non-objective law and fuzzy, evasive, non-objective thinking.

Another part of the bill, Section 584, "Report on the Achievement of Diversity Goals for the Leadership of the Armed Forces," is particularly onerous. It does not even define the term "diversity," but since the term was sired by multiculturalism, one presumes that it means *not* excluding Muslims from command and advisory roles. There are several "prohibitions" or limitations in the bill, but who or what is to enforce them when the bill grants the executive branch, Congress, and bureaucrats the discretionary power to designate who may or may not be an "enemy of the state"?

The U.S. would not be a "battlefield" had we eliminated states that sponsor terrorism over a decade ago. But the Senate bill underscores the fact that our policies do not now and never will identify the specific enemy. This is the deadly neurosis of a nation that has convinced itself that it is not worthy of self-preservation *as a free country*, but as just another "unexceptional" country which must turn on its own citizens to preserve the state and not the rights and liberties America was once famous for.

The police state proposed in S. 1867 needs and requires Americans to be tired, poor, and huddled, but not yearning to be free. Like "The Picture of Dorian Gray," that "beauteous" welfare and regulatory state established early in the 20th century and welcomed by so many, is turning very, very ugly.

*Claire Berlinski, in her article, "Moderate Muslim Watch: How the Term "Islamophobia" Got Shoved Down Your Throat," in November 2011, noted:

Now here's a point you might deeply consider: The neologism "Islamophobia" did not simply emerge ex nihilo. *It was invented, deliberately, by a Muslim Brotherhood front organization, the International Institute for Islamic Thought, which is based in Northern Virginia. If that name dimly rings a bell, it should: I've mentioned it before, and it's particularly important because it was co-founded by Anwar Ibrahim–the hero of Moderate Islam who is now trotting around the globe.*

December 2011

Murder, She Wrote

"If you want a picture of the future, imagine a boot stamping on a human face—forever." — O'Brien to Winston Smith, *Nineteen Eighty-Four**

Politically, mass civil disobedience is appropriate only as a prelude to civil war—as the declaration of a total break with a country's political institutions. — Ayn Rand**

George Orwell's quotation is best underscored with a photo of gloating, laughing Speaker of the House Nancy Pelosi, hefting an over-sized gavel, one allegedly used to hammer semi-socialist Medicare Reform into law, as she lead her fawning boy toys into the House. If you want a picture of America's future, imagine her pounding the faces of Americans with that gavel, or twisting her heel into the face of anyone who opposes her, for the sheer pleasure of it. She looks like a frivolous, mentally light-weight Society matron, but she has the soul of a killer and the shrewdness of a successful gangster. She is the distaff version of Tony Soprano, or of James Taggart of *Atlas Shrugged*, who wanted to hear John Galt scream. It was she who "pressured" Obama and Reid into going for broke, instead of passing health care "reform" piecemeal.

Just who is the actual President of the United States? I can't recall our having elected a matriarch.

And, to clarify Rand's observation – it is President Barack Obama, Pelosi, Senator Harry Reid and every Congressman who voted "Yea," and every Senator who voted for the Senate version of the same bill, who have broken with the country's political institutions to form an illegitimate statist government. The Constitution is quite clear on that matter.

Mass civil disobedience, if it can be communicated and orchestrated, is the proper response to such treason. That treason is represented in the Patient Protection and Affordable Care Act of 2010 (HR 3590), passed by the House on March 21, 10:49 p.m., on a "motion to concur in Senate Amendments." The Democrats squeaked by with a majority of 219 for, 212 votes against. All one hundred and seventy-eight Republicans voted against the bill, and thirty-four Democrats. Readers with strong stomachs may read the proceedings of the 21st here. Readers who wish to go blind or insane reading the bill's full text, may go here.

What is the political institution that has been usurped? A federal government constrained in its powers by the Constitution (before the Sixteenth or income tax amendment, and the Eighteenth Amendment, or Prohibition amendment), limited in its powers over individuals and states, and prohibited from expanding those powers through legislation or the courts.

In short, a government constitutionally fettered in the exercise of its power, but limited in that power to uphold and protect individual rights. And that is all.

Instead, we hear Pelosi crowing about her victory in Sunday's health care vote in the House:

> In doing so, we will honor the vows of our founders, who in the Declaration of Independence said that we are 'endowed by our Creator with certain unalienable rights, that among these are life, liberty and the pursuit of happiness.' This legislation will lead to healthier lives, more liberty to pursue hopes and dreams and happiness for the American people. This is an American proposal that honors the traditions of our country.

One wishes one had the power to prohibit such creatures from quoting thinkers such as Thomas Jefferson, to prevent them from perverting the meaning of the words of their moral and intellectual superiors. Pelosi's intention, however, was to pervert the meaning of the Declaration's principles; make no mistake about that. Of course, there is nothing in the Constitution that mentions "health care" or any Congressional power to legislate for or against it. But words, concepts, and clear meanings are nothing to Pelosi and her co-conspirators in the White House and Congress.

The task now is to educate Americans on that point, and to persuade them to support every effort to repeal and challenge Obamacare in court – as well as support any individual who refuses to comply and is persecuted or rounded up by the government. Americans must be persuaded of the true, evil nature of Pelosi, Reid, Obama and that whole gang. Because that gang has usurped the Constitution in complete contempt of it, of the moral principles underlying it, and of the American people, we no longer have a "representative" government – but a clique of tyrants. This is what we must convince Americans of – enough of them to make a difference.

I find little solace in the Democrats being dethroned in November, which is a virtual certainty. Republicans may replace most of them in the House, but I have no confidence in their ability or motive to oppose Obamacare and get it sliced, diced, or even repealed. More likely, because they share with the Democrats the same altruist premises, they will simply seek to lessen the harsher provisions of the tyranny, such as possibly disconnecting the IRS's expanded power to collect, enforce, and punish.

For as long as the Republicans do not challenge the law on *moral grounds*, they will remain abettors to the crime, as "fiscal conservatives" – as they have always been with Democratically inspired "social legislation" and economic "reform."

Should the Republicans anger the electorate as do-nothing compromisers, the Democrats may find themselves back in the saddle in 2012. Columnist Mark Steyn makes a trenchant observation about why Pelosi and the Democrats do not care if they are massacred next November.

Look at it from the Dems' point of view. You pass Obamacare. You lose the 2010 election, which gives the GOP co-ownership of an awkward couple of years. And you come back in 2012 to find your health care apparatus is still in place, a fetid behemoth of toxic pustules oozing all over the basement, and, simply through the natural processes of government, already bigger and more expensive and more bureaucratic than it was when you passed it two years earlier. That's a huge prize, and well worth a midterm timeout.

In short, the Democrats are not bothered by an electoral ostracism. The little golden treasure box of power goodies will still be there after the Republicans have cursed it but cozened the electorate by leaving all its confiscatory essentials intact, kinder, gentler, but still toxic to individual rights and liberty.

Several states have already passed resolutions, or plan to file lawsuits, citing the 10th Amendment or the right of nullification of federal law, stating that their citizens are not legally required to purchase federally mandated health insurance.

However, it will not be enough for states' attorneys general to file lawsuits against mandatory health insurance, or to cite nullification. They must also challenge the IRS enforcement provisions in the law as part of those suits. If the IRS can threaten to empty an individual's bank account for non-compliance of the law, state law not obliging him to buy federal health insurance will not be much protection. Do not doubt the extent of thuggery Obama et al. have intended this law to reach.

A state's well-intended protection of its citizens against federal taxing power, after all, will be seen as virtual secession. The states would, explicitly or implicitly, be challenging the federal government's power to tax, as stated in the 16th Amendment, ratified in 1913:

> *The Congress shall have power to lay and collect taxes on incomes, from whatever source derived, without apportionment among the several States, and without regard to any census or enumeration.*

This contradicts and undoes Article 1, Section 9 of the Constitution, so carefully and wisely worded by the Founders:

No Capitation, or other direct Tax shall be laid, unless in Proportion to the Census or Enumeration herein before directed to be taken.

Almost tongue-in-cheek, some accounts of the passage of the 16th Amendment claim that the language of that Amendment "clarifies" Article 1, Section 9. Say, rather, obviates it for reasons of state.

A challenge to the mandated purchase of government-approved health insurance must logically and necessarily challenge that taxing power. Non-compliance by an individual in any state would result in a penalty tax. A state might ensure an individual's right to *not* buy the insurance, but would be helpless to prevent that individual from being punished by the federal government. Such resolutions and acts by the states would be as weather vanes blowing in the wind.

So, it is the taxing authority of the federal government that must also be challenged. That event would be earth-shaking, for it would threaten *all* of the federal government's powers to regulate and tax commerce and individuals (as well as the states', counties', and municipalities' own taxing powers). What are the chances of that challenge being made by the states singly or collectively? I do not hold out hope.

Furthermore, most states are dependent on federal funds for highways, education and other subsidized realms. They are addicted to federal assistance. Washington can retaliate by threatening to withhold or deny those subsidies and funds. And the challenge more likely will go poof.

That is one big carrot dangling at the end of the federal two-by-four.

Many of the proposed lawsuits against Obamacare are focusing on the language of the Constitution. One of the more credible arguments is that while Congress may regulate commerce between the states (the term *regulate* meaning something entirely different to the Founders, chiefly that individual state commercial law should have some *uniformity*), how can Congress regulate non-activity or no commerce? Or *cause* the commerce to occur, such as mandating the purchase of health insurance, whether within states or across state lines, and then "regulate" it?

I would believe in the efficacy of such arguments were we not up against a gangster government (thank you, Michelle Bachmann, for that term) to whom words, oaths of office, individual rights, private property, privately *earned* wealth, and constitutional language mean absolutely nothing. This has been so amply and obviously demonstrated by Obama, Pelosi, Reid and their gang that I will not recount the numerous incidents there.

The Supreme Court regained some credibility when it ruled unequivocally in favor of the First Amendment in the *Citizens United* case. Should a challenge to Obamacare ever reach that court, could we count on an encore of that glorious moment? I am placing no bets, especially if Obama has a chance to pack the court after the retirement of Justice John Paul Stevens.

Barack Obama seems to be just a willing stooge, a youngster putty in the hands of a seasoned politician. The Wicked Witch of the West, the Harridan of the House, the Nurse Ratched of what she treats as her own private cuckoo's nest – America – is but one half of the real power behind the throne in the White House. The other half is equally repellent, Rahm Emanuel, chief of staff and professional enforcer.

Bonnie and Clyde, if you will, who boasted that they robbed banks. And committed murder. Oh, I could call Pelosi especially so many more names, few of them printable here.

Orwell's Nineteen Eighty-Four: Text, Sources, Criticism, 1963. New York: Harcourt Brace Jovanovich (1982 edition), p. 178.
**"The Cashing-in: The Student Rebellion," in *Capitalism: The Unknown Ideal*, by Ayn Rand. 1965. New York: Signet, 1967, pp. 256-7.

March 2010

A Summit of Scrambled Egg-Heads

The Colonial Williamsburg Foundation was once dedicated to promoting an understanding of how and why the United States was founded in the 18th century, to communicate a sense of why the Revolution happened. Among its programs was the replication of colonial Williamsburg, once the capital of colonial Virginia, restoring original buildings dating from the period and reconstructing others from extant records.

For decades costumed "interpreters" or actors have roamed the streets of Colonial Williamsburg, regaling visitors with tales and stories from the period, while inside many of the restored or rebuilt structures they introduced visitors to life in the 18th century, from peruke making to 18th century cooking to gardening to the *contradance*. Over its seventy-plus years of existence, Colonial Williamsburg has been explored, toured and experienced by millions of tourists from the United States and from around the world.

All of this was made possible by money from John D. Rockefeller, Jr., who in the 1930's and 1940's invested millions in the resuscitation of what was once a sleepy, down on its luck college town. Less emphasis was put on the explication of the political principles that animated many of the town's more famous residents and visiting burgesses, and more on "life as it was." Which is not to say that visitors did not go away without a better knowledge of George Washington, Patrick Henry, Thomas Jefferson and the rival Randolph and Lee families, to mention a few of the men who once were familiar with Duke of Gloucester Street, the mile-long thoroughfare between the College of William and Mary and the colonial Capitol.

Today, however, in 2007, visitors go away with less of a knowledge of those men, their causes, and their time, and a skewed one, as well – a politically correct one. The rot began to set in and spread late in the last century. What has helped to accelerate the decomposition, among other cultural and political influences, is that Colonial Williamsburg now receives federal money.

When it was a purely private, "not for profit" foundation, depending on donations, endowments, bequests and tourist revenue, it did not need to abide by the Civil Rights Act, or the Equal Opportunity Act, or any other egalitarian legislation intended to usurp and regulate private dealings between individuals and organizations, between employers and employees.

For example, now visitors leave with the impression that there were indeed female footmen and coach drivers, women coopers and carpenters, women fifers and drummers, female "militia persons," and so on, without any attempt by the Foundation or its employees to correct that impression or to even hint at the true, male-defined character of the period.

This is one consequence of taking federal bread – and having to sing the federal song. Accept the federal check, and become politically correct. And it illustrates just one way in which the policymakers of Colonial Williamsburg contradict and ultimately betray the Foundation's decades-old mission and watchword: "That the future may learn from the past." To be willing to falsify the past is to be willing to falsify the present. George Orwell dramatized the motive behind and the consequences of that policy in his novel, *Nineteen Eighty-Four.*

Perhaps worse than falsifying the character of the period, Colonial Williamsburg has hosted several international conferences. Presidents, queens, princes, sheiks, and demagogues have all visited the place in one capacity or another. The latest event was the celebration of the 400th anniversary of the founding of Jamestown in 1607. President and Laura Bush, Queen Elizabeth of England, and other dignitaries all descended on Williamsburg and Jamestown to participate in an orgy of multicultural "diversity" – designed by its organizers to underplay (and in many instances, to diminish or denigrate) the European settlement and overplay or inflate alleged Indian and African cultural contributions.

The climax of the celebration of the beginning of what the Founders more than 150 years later would deem a *republic,* however, will not be a recognition of that unprecedented political feat, but the "World Forum on the Future of Democracy," to take place between September 16 and 18.

According to the August 14th Colonial Williamsburg Newsletter, an employee in-house publication, "The World Forum will bring together noted international and national scholars on democracy, as well as leading government officials, political practitioners, advocates and commentators who have played a role in democracy's advance.

"The signature event of America's 400th anniversary is sponsored jointly by the Jamestown 400th Commemoration Commission, the College of William and Mary, the Colonial Williamsburg Foundation, and the Commonwealth of Virginia's 'Jamestown 2007' organization.

"The Williamsburg Lodge and the College of William and Mary…will both host World Forum events. Invited guests to the World Forum Conference will be given the rare opportunity to hear a distinguished group of international speakers…

> "The first full conference day will focus on [the] 'Architecture of Liberty' and will address the American framers' development of a structure for *deliberative democracy,* the evolution of the

American system over the ensuing centuries, and the contemporary relevance of democracy in a global age." (*Italics* mine.)

I have news for the invited guests, the participants, the chairs, and the panelists of the Forum: the framers did no such thing. What they "structured" was a political system intended to preserve a *republic*, that is, a nation whose government was charged with defending and preserving individual rights against foes foreign and domestic – especially against democratically-inclined domestic ones. The Founders abhorred the idea of a *democracy*, which in history meant mob rule. They knew that democracy, "deliberative" or not, in most cases was an overture to tyranny by mobs or tyranny by dictators. Their papers, correspondence, and speeches bear out that abhorrence. When the Constitution was drawn up for ratification, someone asked Benjamin Franklin what kind of government he and his fellow delegates had created. He answered: "A republic, if you can keep it."

But Americans haven't been able to keep it. They have lost sight of it, or surrendered it in exchange for the messy and expensive pottage of the welfare state. Most do not know the vitally defining differences between a democracy and a republic; to most of them, the terms are synonymous. We have to thank for that appalling and debilitating ignorance a federally dominated public education system dominated by bureaucrats and "educators" one of whose pernicious goals is to convert the study of ideas and the history of ideas into mere "social studies."

Lexicographers have had trouble defining the term *republic*. The common definition of this form of representative government (compiled here from the *Oxford*, *Webster's*, and *American Heritage* dictionaries) usually includes the absence of a monarch as head of state, substituting an elected president or executive, and the right of citizens to elect representatives who are responsible and answerable to the citizens.

However, the political system in the U.S. today meets only half that definition. What elected official is truly held responsible for his actions? Even if he is voted out of office or forced to resign, he can still collect a taxpayer-paid pension and avail himself of taxpayer-paid fringe benefits. He is not answerable for endorsing policies that result in the destruction of individual rights or the seizure of private property or the mortgaging of the lives of the living and the not-yet-born by voting for programs that depend on theft and deficit spending.

The typical politician is privileged to legislate, and indemnified from any ruinous consequences of his actions and policies.

Also, the meaning of the term *republic* has not so much been lost, as ignored. Dictatorships and theocracies have incorporated the term in the names of their slave states, e.g., the Union of Soviet Socialist Republics, the German Democratic Republic, and the Islamic Republic of Iran.

So, in modern practice, the term *republic* has become meaningless. *Democracy*, on the other hand, is what most collectivists and statists prefer to impose in theory and in practice. It means majority rule, or mob rule, even though in many instances the majority may be a fantasy or an illusion of its advocates or of those who believe they are in the majority.

Some notorious instances of democracy in action are: the death of Socrates, the French Revolution, and the election of the Nazi Party to power in Germany. Or, more recently, the democratically elected government of Iraq, which adopted a theocratic constitution, a democracy bought with the lives of thousands of American soldiers. (President Bush's attitude? "So be it, if that's what they want, it was democratically done.") All of these instances of democracy were "deliberated," as well.

Like the defenders of Communism in the past, advocates of democracy contend that the system has been given a bad reputation by artless practitioners or just plain bad luck, that it would be an ideal form of government if only the "right" individuals oversaw its implementation. Its poor and often criminal record is blamed on inconducive circumstances, corruption, and other incidental or irrelevant factors – never on its fundamental nature.

Majority rule, moreover, recognizes no absolute principles necessary to ensure the freedom and legitimate rights of individuals. This was a major concern of the Founders, who, within the limit of their knowledge (which was demonstrably wider and deeper than that of modern politicians), labored to ban *democracy* from the Constitution. Under democracy, absolute principles, founded on the nature of man, are the enemy of the advocates of "social progress" and "political evolution." The rights of minorities, or even the minorities themselves, can be sacrificed for the good of the whole. Or, a minority with political pull can subjugate a majority through the influence of a bloc of ambitious, venal legislators (e.g., the 18th Amendment, or the Volstead Act).

What is *deliberative democracy*, that is, what the Founders *did not* "structure"? One can only guess that it means that instead of instant mob rule, the mob and its leaders stop to talk about it first, to devise the best means of imposing their wishes with the least amount of debate or conflict, before putting individual rights on the tumbrel of legislation for a trip to the guillotine.

The roll call of organizations and individuals participating in the World Forum on the Future of Democracy is largely answered by doe-eyed altruists and professional and career do-gooders. It is complemented by a cohort of political has-beens (such as Charles Robb, former U.S senator from Virginia and its former governor, William P. Barr, 77th Attorney General and now executive vice president and general counsel of Verizon, and retired Supreme Court justice Sandra Day O'Connor), scholars of the people management and one-worlder globalization stripes, and a few odd couples. Leftist news editor and anchor James C. Lehrer of PBS will moderate some of the panels.

Two historians, Gordon Wood of Brown University and Joseph Ellis of Mount Holyoke College, both Pulitzer Prize authors, are also scheduled to appear as speakers and panelists.

The World Forum's list of panel topics is a litany of collectivist causes and statist concerns: "Developing a Structure for Deliberative Democracy – The Framers' Debate" – "Has America Kept the Faith? Is it Working?" – "Are America's Founding Principles Relevant in a Global Age?" – "Terrorism and Security" – "Protecting Religious Freedom and Minority Rights" – "World Markets" – "Sustainable Development."

Among the organizations represented at the Forum are:

➢ The Millennium Challenge Corporation, a U.S. government entity established in 2004, charged with reducing global poverty through the promotion of sustainable growth. It receives an annual Congressional appropriation. "Reducing global poverty" was not what the Founders had in mind when they were "structuring" our alleged democracy. "Sustainable" growth or development, moreover, means the transfer of wealth, private or taxpayer extorted, from a free, prosperous country to an unfree, poor one, as long as the free, prosperous one can sustain its productivity under the twin burdens of regulation and taxation.

➢ The Aspen Institute, which, according to its website, "is an international nonprofit organization dedicated to fostering enlightened leadership and open-minded dialogue…The Institute and its international partners seek to promote nonpartisan inquiry and an appreciation of timeless values." The rest of its mission statement is just as woozily worded and is a pæan to cultural relativism and sensitivity training. One may suppose that political freedom is a "timeless value" appreciated by the principals of the Institute, but is not much defended by them. To defend it as a non-negotiable value would be "close-minded."

➢ CIVICUS, or the "World Alliance for Citizen Participation," dedicated to strengthening citizen action and civil society throughout the world. Its "vision" is "a worldwide community of informed, inspired, committed citizens engaged in confronting the challenges facing humanity." This is also woozy. Perhaps the U.S.-Iranian talks are an example of "civil engagement."

➢ First Peoples Worldwide, "a project of the Tides Center…the only international organization led by Indigenous Peoples and dedicated to the mission of promoting Indigenous economic determination and strengthening Indigenous communities through asset control and the dissemination of knowledge." Which means: keeping the "indigenous" down on the farm and dependent on aid. If these people weren't kept poor, would the do-gooders have anything else to do?

➢ Winrock International, "a nonprofit organization that works with people in the United States and around the world to increase economic opportunity, sustain natural resources, and protect the environment…By linking local individuals and communities with new ideas and technology, Winrock is increasing long-term productivity, equity, and responsible resource management to benefit the poor and disadvantaged of the world." And all those new ideas and the technology come from individuals who fortunately didn't merit Winrock's compassionate attention.

➢ Mortara Center for International Studies (Georgetown University), which apparently specializes in "conflict management" and resolving disputes without passing moral judgment on the conflicting parties. Its mission is "to advance scholarship and inform policy by combining the expertise of scholars and the experiences of international affairs practitioners." The Mortara Center is a creature of Georgetown's School of Foreign Service. Well, look at the sorry record of U.S. diplomacy over the last half-century.

➢ The Cohen Group, a Washington "business" lobby headed by former Secretary of Defense William S. Cohen, and staffed chiefly by high-ranking retired military men. "Our Principals," says its website, "bring centuries of experience [that expression, "centuries of experience," is absolutely meaningless] at the White House, the State Department, the Defense Department, and Congress….The Cohen Group's reach extends internationally where our Principals have developed great expertise and relationships with key political, economic and business leaders and acquired valuable experience with the individuals and institutions that affect our clients' success abroad." One couldn't understate it better. The

shorthand and more honest term for all that expertise and
experience is "political pull." On TCG's website also are several
"success stories," which are nonpareil examples of résumé
padding, puffery, and circumlocution.

Several of the individuals who will appear as speakers or panelists
deserve particular attention.

Carol J. Lancaster, director of the Mortara Center, and currently
teaching courses on political leadership, the politics and economics of
development and ethics, and global development at Georgetown, has made
a career of rationalizing in a scholarly manner the disastrous policy of U.S.
foreign aid.

Jessica P. Einhorn, dean of the Paul H. Nitze School of Advanced
International Studies at the Johns Hopkins University, took that position
after retiring from public careers with the World Bank, the U.S. State and
Treasury Departments, and the U.S. International Development
Corporation Agency. Nominally an "economist," she had stints with the
International Monetary Fund and the Brookings Institute. She is a trustee
of the Rockefeller Brothers Fund and a director of the Institute for
International Economics, the Center for Global Development, and the
National Bureau of Economic Research. This is a "brainy" Hillary Clinton.

Martha Crenshaw is the Colin and Nancy Campbell Professor of
Global Issues and Democratic Thought, and also Professor of Government
at Wesleyan University in Connecticut. (Colin Campbell is president of
Colonial Williamsburg.) She is a kind of scholarly "peacenik." She has
made a career of analyzing and writing about terrorism, but in terms that
treat the subject as a kind of jigsaw puzzle or computer program, *sans* any
moral judgment of terrorists or of states that sponsor terrorism.

She contributed a chapter, "Coercive Diplomacy and the Response to
Terrorism" to a book published by the U.S. Institute of Peace Press, *The
United States and Coercive Diplomacy* and several other papers to
similarly titled works and the quarterly Foreign Affairs. Among her many,
many liberal credits are her memberships on the Committee on Law and
Justice and the Committee on (wait for it!) Determining Basic Research
Needs to Interrupt the Improvised Explosive Device Delivery Chain of the
National Research Council of the National Academies of Science.

Here is a sample of her writing from her article, "Thoughts on
Relating Terrorism to Historical Contexts," in a book she edited, *Terrorism
in Context*. In answer to the question of the consequences of terrorism, she
wrote:

"The impact of terrorism is often lost in a tide of sensational
exaggerations. Furthermore, terrorism shapes interactions among

political actors over long periods of time through a dynamic process in which violence alters the conditions under which it initially occurs. Many consequences are unintended, but it is rare that terrorism (or, more frequently, the government's reaction to terrorism) does not alter political institutions, values, and behavior as well as the functioning of society."

That is her "disinterested" style and perspective, to view terrorism and reactions to it as no better than competing nests of ants that raid each other. One supposes that she regards the reporting of the murder of 3,000 people, mostly Americans, on 9/11, as an instance of sensational exaggeration. Among other things, according to the Wesleyan website, Crenshaw is a former President and Councilor of the International Society of Political Psychology. "Political *psychology*"? Not political *principles*, or political *ideas*?

Which brings me to what initially startled me when I read the list of World Forum participants. Two of the panel topics, mentioned above, are "Terrorism and Security" and "Protecting Religious Freedom and Minority Rights."

Not coincidentally, two individuals who won't be at odds either are retired Coast Guard Admiral James M. Loy, former Deputy Secretary of Homeland Security from 2003 to 2005 (and now senior counselor for The Cohen Group), and Dr. Ingrid Mattson, president of the Islamic Society of North America, and formerly a director of the Islamic Circle of North America.

Loy, who also served as chief operating officer for the Transportation Security Administration, will probably chair or moderate the panel on terrorism and security. He got masters degrees in history/government and public administration from Wesleyan in Connecticut and the University of Rhode Island, and was an intern at the John F. Kennedy School of Government at Harvard. So one can be certain that he will not be saying that President Bush has made a mess of things, that we are losing the so-called "war on terror," and that the solution is to eradicate states that sponsor terrorism – Saudi Arabia, Iran, and Syria.

No, he will probably advocate that to frustrate "radical militants" bent on launching another attack on U.S. soil, the U.S. be turned into a more thorough police state than the DHS and TSA already has, and that we extend a hand of friendship to Islam. Islam, after all, is a "peaceful" religion. Loy would not be a part of the World Forum if he were not soft (or soft-headed) on Islamism, Islamofascism, or whatever other name Islamic jihad goes by.

The Islamic Society of North America claims over two million members. Its affiliated organization, the Islamic Circle of North America, claims near two million members, and Dr. Mattson was also a director of it, as well. These organizations, like CAIR (the Council on American Islamic Relations), MPAC (the Muslim Public Affairs Council), and others that pass as "moderate" or "mainstream" Muslim organizations, practice what can be called "stealth" jihad. (Steve Emerson, an authority on Islamism and jihad, calls this policy "cultural jihad.")

Instead of resorting to violence to punish infidels or send them running into a state of siege (as President Bush has done), American Islamists apply "reverse" assimilation, that is, coaxing or beguiling a host country into accepting Islam on its own terms, terms that are defined by the Koran and Sharia law. To question those terms – indeed, to criticize any facet of Islam – is to risk accusations of "hate speech," racism, bigotry, or religious discrimination or intolerance.

The ISNA, however, is a Saudi-funded militant Islamic group, and preaches the Wahhabist version of Islam. That makes it as bad and as dangerous as CAIR, which in 1993 began as and remains the American branch of Hamas. Neither the Circle nor the Society has hidden its agenda, which is to turn the U.S. into an Islamic nation. For example, the goal of the Circle, stated on its website, is:

> *"...the establishment of Islam in all spheres of life. ICNA has many projects, programs, and activities which are designed to help in the process of molding the individual and reforming society at large."*

The Society's vision, stated on its website, is:

> *"To be an exemplary and unifying Islamic organization in North America that contributes to the betterment of the Muslim community and society at large."*

"Society at large" means all non-Muslims. "All spheres of life" means their conversion to Islam, or their acceptance of the status of dhimmi-hood in a Muslim society.

Mattson, like her colleagues at CAIR and MPAC, presents the "soft face" of militant Islam. Last year she objected to President Bush's use of the term "Islamic fascism." In an Associated Press report of September 1, 2006, she "acknowledged that terrorist groups 'do misuse and use Islamic concepts and terms to justify their violence. But I think that when we then bestow that term upon them we only make the situation worse and somehow give validity to their claims which we need to deny and reject.'"

She probably added, *sotto voce*, "But only for the time being, while we talk these fools into giving us the rope with which we will subjugate or hang them." Mattson got her Ph.D. in Islamic studies from the University of Chicago, which meant, among other things, mastering the art of verisimilitude. The Islamic term for it is *taqiyya*, sanctioned by Mohammed as a means of conquest.

Last year her ICNA also declared itself as being against suicide bombings, except if they are directed against Jews. Mattson doubtless will participate on the "Religious Freedom and Minority Rights" panel.

For an eye-opening panel discussion on the duplicitous means and ends of American Islamic organizations, including those mentioned above, and of the culpability of many of its officials – not to mention the delusions of most of our elected officials and the news media – the reader is directed to a *FrontPageMagazine* article of February 24, 2006, "Victory over Terror?" The chief panelists are Daniel Pipes, Robert Spencer, Steve Emerson, and Phyllis Chesler, all authorities on Islamism and its jihadists, foreign and domestic.

I have not dwelt here on the role of the College of William and Mary as a host for the Forum here, for it is a state university and as guilty as virtually any other school of indoctrinating its students with an anti-Western, anti-American, and anti-reason ideas. Its faculty is largely staffed with teachers of the same philosophical and political ilk of the Forum's participants.

As a measure of how ubiquitous and uncontroversial is the notion in the news media that the U.S. was founded as and intended to be a "democracy," the Newport News *Daily Press*, on September 1, under the headline "The 400th's Last Hurrah," simply wondered if former presidents Bill Clinton and George H.W. Bush, and former British prime ministers Margaret Thatcher and Tony Blair, all designated honorary co-chairs of the Forum, will actually attend.

That is the composition and character of the upcoming World Forum on the Future of Democracy. Given that composition and character, one might have expected the principals of Colonial Williamsburg to view the theme of "democracy" of such a "summit" with opprobrium, and resolve to vigorously discredit its thematic link to Jamestown.

In conclusion, if Colonial Williamsburg is willing to falsify the past, and water down its presentation of the political ideas of the Founders, or filter them through the strainer of political correctness, and see nothing wrong in it – it's just a matter of subjective interpretation, don't you know – it should not be surprising that it would lend its venue to a forum that will promulgate a false state of the world, together with false solutions to perceived or imaginary crises and issues – and see nothing wrong in that, either.

The powers of Colonial Williamsburg do not know the difference between democracy and republicanism – between mob rule and individual rights-based liberty, between a leviathan state and limited government – or do not care to know the difference, as long as Colonial Williamsburg is in the public relations limelight.

September 2007

America's Mobocracy

There are three overlooked or un-emphasized facets of the Obama administration and Congress's breathless rush to seize everything in the country that is not nailed down – health care, car production, the used or "clunker" car market, executive pay – the list may prove to be endless, and there may be nothing that is not nailed down exempt from their avarice. These facets should be the principal foci of critics to the point of obsession.

A minor facet of the Obama administration itself is the Chicago "gangster government" character of his White House staff and his cabinet and departmental appointees. Not all of his appointees are from Chicago. They just have that odor about them, of professional political parasites who have scurried in and out of sight and up and down the totem pole of Washington politics over the years as their chosen career choices, to a soul advancing or pimping for collectivism, most of them never having worked a productive day in their lives. Heading the list is chief-of-staff Rahm Emanuel, who has all the charm and savvy of Meyer Lansky. (One can legitimately wonder if the grandfather of "community organizing," Saul Alinsky, and Lansky traded pointers on political activism. They were Chicago contemporaries.)

The President and his wife, Michelle, of course, live like royalty and behave like it. There are the appointed thirty-two "czars" lording it over the American economy, and then are Michelle's twenty-two staffers who aid her in her "social" life, all of whose salaries are paid by taxpayers – not all of them in Chicago.

The first major facet is that, if there is a crisis in any realm over which the government seeks to expand its power to control, the problem can be traced to government controls in the first place. The minuscule, hardly noticeable controls of yesteryear, when men wore handlebar moustaches and labored to write laws in un-air-conditioned chambers, have grown into a forest of lacerating rose bushes without the benefit of roses. This facet has been admirably dwelt on by better analysts than me, but it has not been emphasized by Tea Party organizers or critics to the level it deserves. It does no good to be preoccupied by cost analyses and projected debt and the like, if they are not accompanied by the moral argument. After all, if mere facts had the power to persuade the minds of our governing elite, why are they so immune to and proof against those facts?

If emails, faxes, hand-written letters, unruly townhall meetings, and demonstrations outside of legislators' offices and the like are beginning to cause some Senators and Congressmen to think twice about the feasibility of their grandiose plans to transform the country from a republic of free individuals to a highly policed and costly hospital regime, forcing them to acknowledge the role of force and fiat law for the "public good" and how that presumptive power has exacerbated existing problems or has simply created them out of whole cloth, ought to underscore the unlikelihood that if they vote for the hospital regime in any form, they in turn will be voted out of office. Our elitist cadre will be obliged to contemplate being forced to make a living in the private sector which they once presumed to "manage," but which their actions have helped to tie into several Gordian knots.

The second facet is that when the White House and Congress prescribe socialism (a.k.a. "progressivism") and legislate to that end, they do it for free. It costs them nothing. They do it with taxpayer money. And, whatever destruction they cause, they are indemnified from the consequences. Ted Kennedy will die without ever having been punished for his crimes. Nancy Pelosi and Barbara Boxer and Henry Waxman will return to California and live the high life on a pension and enjoy health care packages few productive persons could ever afford. Barney Frank and Bernard Bernanke will fade into comfortable retirements and, like Bill Clinton and George H.W. Bush, embark on lucrative speaking careers. Barack and Michelle will traipse back to their Chicago mansion on a pension, as well, and begin to solicit donations for the Obama Presidential Library.

This will ever be a conflict between the "governed" and the government for as long as fiat powers are sanctioned or tolerated by the electorate. It is an unfair contest between the government and the electorate. Those who advocate and pass laws destructive of freedom, property, happiness and the ownership of one's life, work on the money extorted from those who are the subjects or targets of the destructive law. It is time that the thinking electorate woke up to this rigged game and forced the culprits to acknowledge the fact, as well.

Think of it: It cost legislators nothing to regulate or ruin your life. You, on the other hand, must, with countless others, invest time, effort, and money in opposing their plans, besides paying their salaries and getting the check for all their fringe benefits, including first-class health care. And you invest your time, effort and money with no guarantee that it will accomplish anything. Ayn Rand called it the "sanction of the victim." General Patton might liken it to supplying Nazi artillery and Panzer tanks with ordnance with which to blast advancing American forces.

The culprits should be forced to stammer transparent irrelevancies and more obvious lies, and plot to rush undetected from home to office and back again, to avoid being cornered by the citizenry's cattle prods and pitchforks. They should be compelled to feel, for once, powerless, redundant and extraneous. They should be forced to feel mean, small and despised beyond redemption and reclamation.

The third facet concerns the motivation behind all the coercive legislation passed, most recently under the reigns of Bush I, Clinton I, Bush II, and now Bush III (a.k.a. Obama). Tea Partiers should make the key connection between "reform" of the health care system (or of "reform" of anything that attracts a Congressman's attention, for he has nothing else to do in Washington or a state capital or a municipal headquarters but to think up "crises" needing "reform"), and the compulsory nature of such "reform."

Why would politicians bother with "reform" if force were not the key ingredient in the "reform"? There would be no point in their debating "reform" if they did not assume they would have the power to coerce everyone into participating in it. They are not working to extend liberty, but to put fetters on it or to extinguish it altogether. Be warned: Any "compromise" between the Blue Dog Democrats, the Republicans, and the Democrats must by necessity retain the element of coercion, no matter how watered down or conciliatory or "humane" they word the compromise.

Further, the element of coercion or legalized extortion in such legislation should be the main tip-off. Tea Partiers should ask: If the proposed legislation is so efficacious and practical, why, for all the puffery about it being *voluntary*, would it rely on force? Why would its advocates insist that participation be made mandatory? A secondary tip-off is the fact that those proposing or voting for such legislation notably ensure that they are exempt from all its provisions. Organizers should ask themselves: If this idea is so good, why do Congressmen keep their distance from it? Why do they not want to take part in what they wish to force everyone else to participate in? Is there something so seriously wrong with it that they would no more want to buy it than they would a used car from Richard Nixon?

Yes. There is something wrong with it. The element of force guarantees its impracticality and its character as a moral and economic fraud – just as robbing a bank or a 7-11 is immoral and an impractical way to "make a living." Waxman, Pelosi, Dodd, Obama, Frank and the rest of the "progressive" crew, all know this. They are not idiots. The only village idiots party to the fraud are those members of the news media who shill for the plan with looks of urgency – an urgency that does not dwell on the insidiously evil aspects of the plan, chief among which are its compulsory provisions.

August 2009

Review: *Fascism and Theater*

 T he first time I watched a political convention to nominate and select presidential and vice-presidential candidates – I forget whether it was a Democratic or Republican one, it hardly mattered then, and does not matter now – I was astounded and not a little appalled by the sheer mindlessness of the event. There they were, hundreds of party delegates from all the states, a great slobbering mass worked up into consecutive bouts of noisy, frenzied rapture over supposedly charismatic nonentities whose platforms and speeches were measures of carefully crafted banality and skillfully inserted buzz words.

There they were, hundreds of adults of both sexes and various ages and sizes, wearing buttons and masks and funny hats and other goofy party paraphernalia, shouting and cheering themselves hoarse on cue in unison, forming conga lines and waving flags and signs, behaving as though they had all checked their brains, dignity and self-respect at the door. Which they evidently had. It was politics as a football game, it was a life-and-death matter of "our team" versus "their team" – all ideational content abandoned and replaced by raw emotion triggered by faces associated with particular sounds emptied of meaning.

The capacity for abandoning one's mind and for taking orders from delegate leaders has always seemed to be an important qualification for being a convention delegate. On the convention floor a delegate was and is still expected to surrender his "autonomous inner man" or individuality and merge into a smothering, communal *gestalt* with his party colleagues.

It is well known that television game show guests and contestants are selected for their quotient of enthusiasm and ability to communicate it to and with an audience. By this measure, a political convention has any game show beat by a factor of a thousand. And the prize is not a fancy car or living room set or a Caribbean cruise or $100,000, but the White House and "our guy" sitting in the Oval Office. In such escapist moments, when delegates seem to undergo a kind of mass "out of body" experience, the candidate is reduced to a mere symbolic image, regardless of character or qualification. He is "it." They become human counterparts of Pavlov's dogs, able to bark and drool and froth at the mouth on command and at the slightest autosuggestion by an overbearing delegate whip.

This is "democracy" in action. It was and still is stage-managed theater. It has not changed at all from the first time I saw a convention on black and white television. Being caught in the middle of such a phenomenon would be as scary to me as being surrounded by a mob of Muslims carrying signs that read "Behead those who insult Islam." One would be tempted to strike out at the maddened, sweating fools on the convention floor, only at the risk of being pummeled to death by delegates from Wisconsin and Idaho and Massachusetts and California. They would all plead temporary insanity, and get away with it.

After all, you had insulted their candidate, their Mahdi, their Thirteenth Imam. Their Savior. You deserved to die.

The religious hysteria, as an element of the phenomenon, is not coincidental, or an anomaly, or a fluke. It is part and parcel of modern convention behavior. It clearly was not a governing factor of the Constitutional Convention of 1787. Then, delegates brought their brains with them; they brought their principles and rectitude. Can you imagine the Founders wearing funny hats and chanting slogans and forming conga lines to press a point of Constitutional law? No? Is the contrast too ludicrous and obscene to contemplate? Yes. Each and every one of those men, even the villains and fence-sitters, was an exemplar of intellectual and moral decorum. Then look at the baboons and halfwits who are charged with selecting an individual whom they want to "run the country." Their choices over the last half century or more are reflections of what transpires on convention floors.

Today, the catalyst for the hysteria is not an invisible deity, but a flesh-and-blood human being. With calculated "behavioral" conditioning (*à la* B.F. Skinner), and a willingness to submerge one's identity in the collective, the sight and sound of a candidate can reduce these delegates to quivering masses of raw emotion. One almost expects them to fall to the convention floor, wreathing and shrieking in deliverance, and speaking in tongues like any Holy Roller. Call it Political Pentecostalism.

Reading *Fascism and Theatre: Comparative Studies on Aesthetics and Politics of Performance in Europe, 1925-1945**, I was not surprised to find in this collection of essays similarities between the methods employed by Nazis, Fascists and Communists to create and sustain support for their régimes, and the methods by which the Democrats and Republicans recruit and maintain their hard core, registered voters, activists and especially their convention delegates, the ones charged with nominating their parties' candidates – that is, the people responsible for foisting onto this country for the last half century or more a succession of fork-tongued demagogues and empty suits.

There are eighteen chapters in *Fascism and Theatre*, but only a few can be highlighted here. Some deal with the subject more successfully than others, but all discuss the role of "theater" in fascism. The term *fascism* is used generically in the essays to stand for Mussolini's Italian Fascism, Hitler's Nazism, and, to a lesser extent, General Francisco Franco's Falangist or Nationalist régime, which was a tepid admixture of Fascism and Nazism. (Although Spain remained "neutral" during World War II,

Franco approved of sending approximately 19,000 Spanish volunteers to serve in a special division of the German army, to fight exclusively the "Bolsheviks" on the Eastern Front, but not the forces of Western armies. Spanish troops fought with the SS during the Soviet taking of Berlin.)

The term *theater* as used in the essays means either extravagant mass events such as the annual Nuremberg rallies or the political subornation of high and popular culture, from operas to plays to folk festivals to suit or conform to fascist aims and purposes.

One indisputable characteristic of fascism is that its theater borrowed heavily from Christian and especially Catholic practices and rituals, selectively exploiting the emotional nature of religion. Roger Griffin, in "Staging the Nation's Rebirth," introduces this idea which is elaborated on in most of the other essays:

> ...[F]ascism, if it can seize power, is able to remain true to its core myth and legitimate itself only by generating an elaborate civic liturgy (or a 'civic,' or 'political' religion) based on the myth of imminent national rebirth. In the two cases where it managed to conquer the State, it rapidly developed characteristic rites and ceremonial, its own iconography and symbology, its own semiotic discourse, aping (but only aping) any established Church. [p. 25]

For Hitler and Germany, "rebirth" meant the resurrection of a Teutonic or Aryan state superior to all, and to rise from the ashes of the Versailles Treaty and the failed Weimar Republic; for Mussolini and Italy, it meant reviving the imperial grandeur of ancient Rome. Hitler and Mussolini, however, had first to concoct and propagate "myths" about the lost greatness of their countries, and then pose as saviors or messiahs who alone had the power to reclaim the greatness and lead their nations to glory. Propaganda ministries and bureaucracies were created in both countries to establish and enforce official party lines about a nation's past, present and future the subjects of art or in plays, national holidays, and even in opera.

Much of editor Günter Berghaus's contribution to the collection of essays, "The Ritual Core of Fascist Theatre: An Anthropological Perspective," is flawed by psycho-babble and sociological semiotics, but much of it also is lucid and on-point. To wit:

> Fascist parties rose to positions of power by gaining mass support and winning democratic elections. Millions of people were inspired by Mussolini and Hitler and developed a genuine enthusiasm for their politics, because they promised an answer to a need that was widely felt in different sections of the population.

People were fascinated by what fascism proposed in response to a crisis that affected the economic, social and cultural spheres of their lives. Political promises played a role in this, but the *emotional appeal* of the leaders and their programs was probably stronger. Fascist leaders avoided the *rational rhetorics* typical of bourgeois politicians, and instead employed *performative language* that had a captivating force unequalled by traditional means of propaganda. {pp. 39-40. *Italics* mine.]

Sound familiar? Does that passage hark back to the 2008 presidential campaign and election? Does it not describe the method by which the current occupant of the White House rose to power? However, Berghaus correctly dwells on the relationship between the religious and secular elements of fascism.

This grafting of the Christian redeemer and savior image onto a historical person was a post-figuration technique often employed in the Christian drama of the Baroque period and was ultimately derived from medieval theology. Both Hitler and Mussolini were well versed in the literary traditions of Christian religion and were fully capable of adopting their conventions. Hitler helped the transformation of his own person into the archetypal, divine redeemer figure through his mythological biography, *Mein Kampf.* [p. 62]

Berghaus quotes Hitler on the purpose of the Party rallies held in Nuremberg and other German cities. From *Mein Kampf.*

Mass meetings are a necessity because the individual (…) who feels isolated and easily succumbs to the fear of loneliness, is given here an idea of a greater community. (…) When he as a seeker is swept along by the mighty effect of the ecstasy and enthusiasm of three to four thousand others, when the visible success and agreement of thousands confirm to him the rightness of the new doctrine (…), then he will submit to the magic spell of what we call "mass suggestiveness." The will, the longing, as well as the power of thousands of people are accumulated in every individual. The man who entered such a meeting doubting and wavering leaves it with an inner conviction: he has become a member of a community. [p. 60]

One could also say that this was no less true for Hitler, that he was literally nothing if not the leader of such a community. Without all those chanted "Sieg Heils" and tens of thousands looking up at him on a high rostrum with adoration and worship, he was a vacuum, an isolated and fearful nonentity who assumed an identity only in the presence and eyes of disciplined and attentive mobs.

Many uninvolved contemporary observers were struck by the fact that the public rituals of fascist régimes were "more than a gorgeous show; [they] also had something of the mysticism and religious fervor of an Easter or Christmas mass in a great cathedral." "Is this a dream or reality?" asked one of the visitors to the *Reichsparteitag* 1936 after the spectacle on the Zeppelinwiese and concluded: "It is like a majestic church service (*Andacht*) where we have congregated to find new strength..."

> [Albert] Speer said that Hitler canonized the formations, processions and celebrations so that "they were almost like rites of the founding of a Church." Once he had worked out the right forms, he wanted to fix them as "unalterable rites" that gave him the status of a "founder of a religion." [p. 53]

Mussolini was of a like mind concerning the religious "experience" possible in the Italian version.

> Mussolini stated in 1923 that "Fascism is a religious phenomenon of vast historical proportions" and that fascism was "a civic and political belief, but also a religion, a militia, a spiritual discipline, which has had – like Christianity – its confessors, its testifying witnesses, its saints." The Fascist Party was often described as "a new Church (*La nuova chiesa* is the title, for example, of a play by [Virgilio] Caselli) or as a "religious or military order." [pp. 53-54]

For example, from 1933 on, from Hitler's assumption of the chancellorship through the next eleven or so years, German playwrights (those who prostituted their talents to the Party) wrote plays that portrayed the past struggle of the German people to assume their "rightful" place in the world. If this meant fudging history or ascribing to past historical persons presaging yearnings for Nazi or Fascist domination and identity, such hacks were perfectly willing to falsify history, submit their work to Party censors and make the requisite changes. As Berghaus notes:

> Consequently, fascist playwrights evoked a large number of situations that indicated a return to a united people. They propagated a new ethics that was aimed at *overcoming egotism*, uniting one individual with other individuals, creating a firm bond between them, making them identify with the aims of the fascist

State and submit to the orders of a leader....The conduct of this
leader was modeled, of course, on the historical examples given by
the Führer, Duce, and Caudillo. Or rather, one should say, on the
way those historical figures were mythisised, legendised and
sanctified in fascist hagiography. [p. 61. *Italics* mine.]

Neither Hitler nor Mussolini was ever portrayed in these plays.
Some species of false but more likely fearful fastidiousness in Party
censors prohibited it; no actor could have been trusted to faultlessly
impersonate Hitler or Mussolini, even had a hack written a play that
featured them, and probably no actor would have wished to risk the role,
either. Hitler and Mussolini were instead substituted with stand-ins or
proxies, such as Frederick the Great or Bismarck or Garibaldi or some
two-dimensional fictional character, always ready to sacrifice himself for
the greater good in the most cavalierly selfless manner, which was the
unity of the German or Italian people. Acceptable plays were set in the
past, to convey a false historical overture to Nazism or Fascism – or the
alleged inexorable inevitability of Nazism and Fascism, which a mere
individual was helpless to oppose and whose only recourse was to submit
to it.

Barbara Panse, in her essay, "Censorship in Nazi Germany: The
Influence of the Reich's Ministry of Propaganda on German Theater and
Drama, 1933-1945," discusses several of these plays, and cites how one
playwright even perverted the American Revolution:

In Hanns Johst's play [*Thomas Paine*], Thomas Paine is the
ideological Führer of the American War of Independence. He, too,
upholds the notions of colonialism and conquest. With the
propagandistic slogan, "America needs land," he seeks to mobilize
the exhausted and hungry insurgent army so that they venture to
take the path into the unknown, to victory or death. His appeal to
faith and comradeship forges the "racially worthy citizens"
(*volkisch wertvollen Glieder*) of America into a nation. In this
play, the life of the Führer character also ends tragically, but his
mission is fulfilled: the 'national idea' has come to fruition. [p.
149]

Johst wrote this play in 1927. He was a career anti-Semite who
wrote a play, *Schlageter*, which extolled Nazi ideology, to celebrate
Hitler's victory and birthday in 1933. It is interesting to note also that
Howard Fast, a steadfast member of the American Communist Party, also
appropriated the American Revolution as a means to advance the "people's
struggle" narrative (*à la* Howard Zinn) on the origins of the United States.

Citizen Tom Paine (1943) is one of a number of novels he wrote set in that period.

No discussion of the theatrics of fascism would be complete without mentioning Leni Riefenstahl's documentary, *Triumph of the Will.* This task fell to contributor Hans-Ulrich Thamer and his essay, "The Orchestration of the National Community: The Nuremberg Party Rallies of the NSDAP." Writing about the purpose and style of the rallies, Thamer observes about the 1934 Nazi Party Congress:

> The heroic style and dramaturgy of the event were fixed on celluloid by Leni Riefenstahl in her film *Triumph of the Will* (1934). Much more than simply a documentary, this film foregrounded the symbolism and liturgy of the ceremonies and established their pattern for the years to come. At the same time, the film disseminated the mass spectacle of Nuremberg throughout Germany. It was a "production of a production" and thereby a reduplication of the "mass appeal" of National Socialist political aesthetics. *Triumph of the Will* turned the military parade of the National Socialist movement into a platform for the Führer-cult. [p. 175]

Thamer then takes the reader on a tour of the typical succeeding rallies, all based on what Riefenstahl had recorded in 1934, which acted as a template, and then were expanded in scope and in the number of participants. These rallies lasted for days. Thamer follows Hitler from elevated rostrum to a ceremony of flags and banners when he rubbed shoulders and pressed flesh with rank-and-file, to a ritual of consecration of the "martyrs" that was much like a glorified mass of the dead. Hitler was the focal point of every important event. But, it was all a manufactured show.

> Nothing was left to chance in the stage-management of the Nuremberg rallies. Every stylistic device had a purpose. The flags were determined in number, size and position; shortcomings in the urban development and gaps in the old town fortifications were covered up by scenery. Everything was subjected to the meticulous plans of the bureaucratic and technical apparatus. The men in charge of the cult were cool-headed technicians, sons of a rational era. Yet they were also theatrical wizards who knew intuitively how to exploit age-old cultic practices for their political aims. It was exactly this link between atavistic ideology, mystical ceremony and the modern age, which helped to *eliminate all*

critical reasoning in both audience and participants. [p. 186. *Italics* mine.]

Before the entire length of *Triumph of the Will* was removed from YouTube for copyright infringement (the full version now can be watched with ads), I watched it twice, and I can attest to the effectiveness of the stage management described by Thamer. I distinctly remember Jimmy Carter's appearance at the conclusion of the 1976 Democratic Convention, when he and his wife Rosalind appeared on stage before a brilliant blue background. That was calculation.

The typical American political convention is also planned and laid out in meticulous detail, from the flags and bunting, to the timed applause and cheers, to the demonstrations of dancing and chanting, to the bands and choreography and lighting, all the way to the climax of the acceptance speeches. Little during these cattle calls could be called spontaneous, except for the essential emotional character of the proceedings that verges on a mass revival meeting. But the spontaneity is also cued and calculated to advance or obstruct a point of order or dissension. For the typical delegate, a convention is a vacation from reality, from the facts of political and economic life.

I doubt that many delegates, upon returning home from a *Grand Gestalt*, pause long enough to acknowledge just how much they have degraded themselves and regret having let loose a monster. And the ensuing political campaigns have become more and more shallow and meaningless popularity contests, with candidates stooping to the level of rock stars repeating the most popular lyrics and buzz words. Thamer concludes his essay with:

> The Führer-myth as the propagandist core of the rally distracted from the political reality of Party as well as everyday life and became the most important means of stabilizing the rule of the Nazi Party. The dream world conjured up by the events manipulated consciousness and created a second reality, which of course could not change the outside world, but could counteract and control it. [p. 188.]

The Obama/McCain campaigns of 2008 were also products of such dream worlds, the one more masterfully managed and staged than the other. And then the winner encountered the "outside world" and, like King Canute, as the legend goes, he attempted to command its tides to cease. In fact, Canute was making a point for his supporters, that he was only a king and not a miracle worker. Perhaps Obama will be imbued with the same wisdom. He must know by now that he's exhausted his distraction skills.

The Republicans, however, seem determined to offer their own Æthelred the Unready to oppose him. Election year 2012 is going to be interesting.

*Providence/Oxford: Berghahn Books: 1996. Edited by Günter Berghaus.

December 2011

Islam

The Ruses of Domestic Islamic 'Rage' Against Freedom of Speech

"We can look as far back as the 1930's in the years prior to the Holocaust when Nazi Germany circulated hate-filled images of our Jewish brothers and sisters throughout society...It is necessary for all of us to stand together and speak out against this, as hatred does not discriminate against any color, race, creed, or religion; all it does is hate."

No, this was not an appeal written by a Jewish person to protest the abominable depiction of Jews in Arab newspapers and on Arab news media. It was written by Maheen H. Farooqi, President of the Islamic Center at New York University in a broadcast email alert to the school's Muslims about the display of the Danish Mohammed cartoons during a panel discussion on them at the university on March 29th, and to organize a demonstration against the event.

NYU President John Sexton caved in to pressure from this group and announced that if the cartoons were displayed, the event must be closed to the public, and only "members of the NYU community" would be allowed to hear the panel discussion. Subsequently, not only was there a demonstration by Muslim students, but many of them bought tickets to the event and destroyed them in an effort to limit attendance.

Meanwhile, in the real world of book retailing, Borders and its affiliate Waldenbooks have banned a forthcoming issue of "Free Inquiry" from their magazine racks because that number of the periodical will feature inside it some of the Danish cartoons. Cited were a fear of violence from radical Muslims and a desire to ensure the safety of the chain's employees and customers.

Creeping socialism. Stealthy statism. The slippery slope of censorship and "responsible" public policy, also known as self-censorship. Someone please correct me, but I believe that Ayn Rand once remarked that at the rate the West is deteriorating, it will not end with a bang, but with a burp. The foregoing instances of submission to Islamic threats and pressure are warnings and guarantees of more to come.

If you have not already noticed it, endorsement of the display of the Danish cartoons – indeed, any expression of criticism about Islam – is steadily being equated with racism, hatred, and discrimination. And not only that, but Mr. Farooqi has the unmitigated but apparently effective gall to assert a "bond" with "our Jewish brothers and sisters." His email "call to arms" is too long to reprint here, but it is chock full of gems.

The Holocaust? Does not Mr. Farooqi know that the president of Iran, Adolf Ahmadinejad, has denied that it ever occurred?

"We, however, would not encourage racism is (sic) any shape or form, and to us and many others, these cartoons are racist and we adamantly oppose their display."

So, don't look at them. No, that's too easy advice to follow. It's almost as though he and his protest organizers want to see them in order to whip the Muslim masses into a window and skull breaking lather. In order to frighten cowards like John Sexton into capitulating to their "demands." In order to impose censorship.

Oh, no, we don't want to impose censorship! Allah forbid!

"The event itself and the topic that the students would like to discuss is not problematic in any way, but the pictures themselves are just hatred and there is (sic) no justification in preaching something breeds that kind of hate."

So, Mr. Farooqi and his "brothers and sisters" won't mind a panel discussion of the cartoons, so long as the subject is not present, if it is unseen, invisible. Excuse me, but that ultimatum is problematic. If the subject of the discussion cannot be shown or displayed, what is it, then, that would be discussed? An abstraction that had no anchor in reality. It would be tantamount to a court trying a murder case but declaring all evidence of it inadmissible. And if the subject has already been deemed "hateful," why discuss it at all?

What a formula for shutting down men's minds for fear of provoking irrational emotional outbursts and threats to one's life! What an appeal to submit to unreason!

And what an excuse for Mr. Sexton, Borders, the Wall Street Journal and others to turn tail and betray the First Amendment! With allies like them, who needs Islam to imperil the Bill of Rights?

But the chief interest here is the stress Mr. Farooqi and his colleagues at CAIR and other Islamic organizations are beginning to put on race, hatred and discrimination. Now, Islam is a set of ideas (if a random set of injunctions to kill or enslave infidels, together with contextless homilies, can be said to be a set of "ideas"), and to oppose it or criticize it is not synonymous with "racism." Aside from the fact that numerous Caucasians, blacks and Asians have converted to Islam, it is beyond anyone's power to deny that most Muslims are of Mideastern Semitic or of other large racial stocks. All intelligent, rational criticism of Islam has been targeted at the nature of the creed and its agenda of conquest, together with the fact that most jihadists and suicide bombers have been and will continue to be Muslim.

Consider also the near conversion to a saccharine Islam of the Canadian "peace worker" hostages who, upon release, did not thank the American, British and Canadian soldiers who freed them, and whose statements lead one to believe that they would have been perfectly willing to remain hostages until they rotted. Their selflessness was in the same league as any suicide bomber's. Or consider the statements and behavior of American journalist Jill Carroll, who upon her release by her captors began spouting sympathy for the *mahujadeen* (Islamic warriors) who were only "defending their country against occupation" and who flaunted Muslim female dress.

It is those *mahujadeen*, otherwise known as "insurgents," who are killing her fellow countrymen and thousands of the Iraqis she purported loves.

Were these former Western hostages brainwashed in captivity? No. To judge by their portrayals in Western news media before they were taken hostage, they were already selfless airheads, susceptible to conversion to Islam. Mr. Farooqi wrote:

> "These same cartoons unfortunately have lead to riots, protests, beatings, and deaths all round the world."

And all that carnage, together with the burning of Western embassies and the fatwas against the Danish cartoonists, who have gone into hiding, has been the handiwork of whom? Whose violence was being committed?

That of Muslims – Sunnis, Shi'ites, and other sects of that mind-suffocating, tongue-severing creed were the ones on the rampage.

Most Americans – indeed, most Caucasian Westerners – wouldn't know a Muslim unless he announced the fact.

Do the cartoons foster hatred? It is healthy and life-preserving to hate something that is inimical to one's freedom of speech and thought. But the cartoons do not foster hatred. They are mildly amusing; some are incomprehensible.

Islam, however, doesn't want anyone to be amused by Mohammed. It wants men to fear him and obey his Allah, just as Winston Smith in Orwell's "Nineteen Eighty-Four" was expected to fear, revere, and love Big Brother. Otherwise, how could anyone submit to his will? In that great film comedy, *His Girl Friday*, Cary Grant as Walter Burns shouts to his page editor over the phone: "Take Hitler and stick him on the funny pages!" That's where Mohammed truly belongs, in the comics, in the company of Hagar the Horrible and the Wizard of Id. Or in a Monty Python movie. When was the last time a Scandinavian suicide bomber blew up a Christian church because Leif Erickson and the Vikings were the subject of humor?

Is dislike or fear of Islam discriminatory? Discrimination is anyone's right, especially when it entails discriminating against mysticism and anyone who threatens physical force or terror in its name. Discrimination in this instance is not a matter of race or hatred, but of reason-based revulsion for a degrading, freedom-crushing creed.

No, the accusations of racism, hatred and discrimination are merely ruses, or straw men, employed to deflect attention away from Islam's goal of suppressing any and all criticism of it, to frighten men from any thought of opposing it lest they be accused of those things.

In the case of NYU and Borders, it worked. As a reward, alumni and corporations should refuse to donate money to NYU, and the school's trustees should fire Sexton. And Borders and Waldenbooks should be subjected to a national boycott until its finds the courage to exercise its right of freedom of speech.

And the cartoons should be proudly and fearlessly displayed.

March 2006

"Honor" Killings: East Meets West

Two kinds of death are the subject here, and they are related in their fundamental means and ends.

The University of Delaware was recently caught *flagrante delicto* in an attempt to kill the selves of its seven thousand students. As the Foundation for Individual Rights in Education (FIRE) reported on its own site (and as reported on numerous other sites, but not much in the mainstream press, if at all), the University announced a campus-wide program of what I would call the nazification of its student body ("University of Delaware Requires Students to Undergo Ideological Reeducation," October 30). (See "None Dare Call It Indoctrination" on The Dougout site, and "Indoctrinating Green Warriors" on this site.)

Others would call it brainwashing, or indoctrination. The North Vietnamese Communists "struggled" recalcitrant citizens until they not only submitted to the Party line, but actively promoted it, as well, as the sole mark of redemption. The University referred to the program as "treatment," as though anyone passing through the school's portals was *ipso facto* mentally ill and in need of getting "his mind straight" until he was certifiably politically *corrected* and converted into an activist robot (or, according to the mission statement, a "change agent"). Which meant being reduced to the mental and intellectual level of Winston Smith at the end of Orwell's *Nineteen Eighty-Four.* Smith began by hating Big Brother, and ended by loving him, a state reached partly by torture and brutal persuasion by his tormenter, O'Brien, and partly by surrender.

While the O'Briens of the University of Delaware may omit the physical torture, the effect on morally and intellectually disarmed young persons can be the same.

> "The Orwellian program," reported FIRE, "requires the approximately 7,000 students in Delaware's residence halls to adopt highly specific university-approved views on issues ranging from politics to race, sexuality, sociology, moral philosophy, and environmentalism. The Foundation....is calling for the total dismantling of the program, which is a flagrant violation of students' rights to freedom of conscience and freedom from compelled speech."

Since being exposed, the University of Delaware has suspended the program, but may try to revive it when its academic O'Briens think no one is looking. Every one of the issues students are expected to absorb and agree with is governed by anti-reason, anti-man, anti-individualist ideas.

"The university's views," reported FIRE, "are forced on students through a comprehensive manipulation of the residence hall environment, from mandatory training sessions to 'sustainability' door decorations. Students living in the university's eight housing complexes are required to attend training sessions, floor meetings, and one-on-one meetings with their Resident Assistants (RAs)."

There is also the matter of the RAs wielding the power of extortion if their reports on students are included the students' academic records. If a student knows that if he does not demonstrate that he is a "team player" or not voluble enough in his "diversification" training or puts an "offending" poster on his dorm door, he might find his grades lowered and his record compromised. But that is a minor issue compared with the evil that is imposed on him.

The major issue is that the program was specifically designed to obliterate the self (or ego) of the individual student, so that the student becomes a mindless cell of a pliable collective, committed to, among other things, reducing his "carbon footprint," demonstrating for the "oppressed" group of the moment, and campaigning for a "sustainable world," with no questions asked or permitted. If the O'Briens have done their job, questions would not even be possible in the victim.

That is one form of "honor killing," that is, a major educational institution acting to enforce a pandemic of irrational, nihilistic ideas that it believes are "pro-life, pro-earth," but which in fact are destructive of life, liberty and ultimately of one's existence. One might, for argument's sake, contend that the university officials who designed the program were ignorant of the consequences of the ideas they wish to enforce. The only valid response to that question would be counter-question: Then what are they doing running a university, if they are so ignorant and so foolishly hostile?

But the creatures who designed the "treatment" program at the University of Delaware were not the Three Stooges. They cannot plead ignorance or stupidity or foolishness. They intended to kill whatever surviving, crippled sense of self students brought with them to the university after enduring milder versions of such indoctrination in middle and high school, just as Ellsworth Toohey cultivated, exploited, and ultimately killed the precarious sense of self in Peter Keating in Ayn Rand's *The Fountainhead.*

"Just say that reason is limited," says Toohey to Keating. "That there's something above it. What? You don't have to be too clear about it either. The field's inexhaustible. 'Instinct' – 'Feeling' – 'Revelation' – 'Divine Intuition' – 'Dialectic Materialism.' [To which one might add today: 'Community service' – 'Volunteerism' – 'Environmentalism' – 'Global society.'] If you get caught at some crucial point and somebody tells you that your doctrine doesn't make sense – you're ready for him. You tell him that there's something above sense. That here he must not try to think, he must *feel*. He must *believe*. Suspend reason and you play it deuces wild. Anything goes in any manner you wish whenever you need it. You've got him. Can you rule a thinking man? We don't want any thinking men."

Neither, apparently, does the University of Delaware. If honor, as Rand defined it, is self-esteem made visible in action, then the university's program was planned to *dishonor* its students by killing their self-esteem and turning them into compliant ciphers, ready to submit to any "higher cause" and prepared, as a way of life, to wage war on those who do not submit. It would never occur to such students that there is no honor in selflessness. Such a conclusion would require thought.

There is an eerie similarity between the means and ends of the University of Delaware's "reeducation" program and what happens to anyone who violates the "community" standards in the Mideast. The Sunday *Times* (London) of November 4th carried a horrendous story, "'Honour' killings grow as girl, 17, stoned to death." And the "moral" barbarity the article describes is essentially what the nihilists in the West wish to reduce everyone to.

The "honor" killings are centered on the violation of Islamic social mores (one can hardly call them a philosophy, they are so concrete bound) when an unmarried woman develops a real or imagined relationship with a man not approved by his family or tribe. "According to the human rights ministry in northern Iraq, 598 women have been burnt, beaten, shot, strangled, thrown from tall buildings, force-fed with lethal drugs, crushed by vehicles, drowned, decapitated, or made to kill themselves so far this year, exceeding the 553 recorded for the whole of 2006."

In this instance, Du'aa, a 17-year-old girl, member of a bizarre non-Muslim sect, the Yazidi (a creed composed of elements from Christianity, Judaism, Islam, and minor faiths and as old as Islam itself) was found together with her 19-year-old Sunni Muslim boyfriend. Muslims are forbidden to marry outside Islam, but the pair was determined to be married.

> "They were not lovers, though some in the crowd suspected they were. But Du'aa was a member of the Yazidi sect, which teaches that the Earth is in the care of seven angels. Yazidis are regarded as devil-worshippers by many Muslims and Muhannad is a Sunni Muslim."

It did not help that the Yazidis believe that Allah or God does not govern the earth, but is "uninvolved," leaving the governance to seven angels lead by a repentant Satan himself. Those and other beliefs of the Yazidis are abhorrent to Muslims. But the Yazidis share the same foolish notion of "honor" as the Muslims. When a local Yazidi sheik surrendered her to the mob for punishment, Du'aa was taken to the marketplace, "in a headlock, wailing and screaming as armed police watched in silence," and stoned to death. The deathblow was delivered by a cousin, who smashed her head with a piece of concrete, purportedly as an act of mercy. Several other of her cousins also participated in the stoning.

The *Times* article relates that "one of the most shocking things about Du'aa's death, however, is that although stoning is rare, honour killing is rampant, particularly in Kurdish areas of Iraq and Iran. Kurdish women are killed almost every day for 'dishonouring' their families."

The "self-esteem" of such barbarians – dependent on what family members and neighbors think of them, measured by primitive concepts that form an irrational, eclectic moral code – is linked to preserving some collectivist sense of "honor." An unmarried woman seen alone with a man not her relative automatically commits a "sin," which "sin" must be blotted out by blotting out her life. Her family's "honor" is thus restored.

Incidentally, it is this kind of culture which University of Delaware students would have been expected to withhold judgment of in the name of "diversity." "Silence is consent," states the school's agenda for lobotomizing its white students in regards to racism. But that statement is meant to be a double-edged sword; "silence" on the subject of Kurdish honor killings can be taken as approval, and earn high marks from a student's RA.

This is the rule in all Islamic countries, one which Islamic activists are quietly campaigning to introduce and have gain "respect" and acceptance in secular Western nations, notably Europe.

It is this kind of non-thinking tribal mentality which programs such as the University of Delaware's seek to inculcate in Western students. In such graduates, it would be but a short step from "honor harassment" of smokers, non-recyclers, and others who refrain from joining the "community" or submitting to its standards, to literal honor killings in the role of "change agents."

We see a form of this kind of violence in the attacks on abortion clinics and in the destruction of private property by environmentalists. Skeptics of anthropogenic global warming have been fired, harassed, and threatened with violence or the ruin of their careers by the enforcers of *belief* in the theory.

I make no distinction between the murder of Du'aa committed by her cousins and the murder of the egos of any student at the University of

Delaware or in any other educational venue, be it kindergarten, grade, middle and secondary schools, or college. The head-bashing concrete can take either form, with the only difference in result being immediate or prolonged death.

November 2007

Islam's Viral Stasis

Two recent, contrasting analyses of Islam – or rather, of the Islamic "mindset" that governs the behavior of Muslims – help to identify the problem with the ideology. One is "Why Muslim cultures lag behind," by "Anti-Jihadist" on Robert Spencer's Jihad Watch. The second is by Daniel Greenfield on Sultan Knish, "Will Islam Destroy Itself?" Both articles discuss what can be described as Islam's state of stasis, or moral, political, and cultural stagnation. The *Merriam-Webster Dictionary* best indicates the phenomenon:

> **Stasis**: a: a state of static balance or equilibrium; stagnation b: a state or period of stability during which little or no evolutionary change in a lineage occurs

That Islam fosters stagnation in its adherents' cultures is an observable given. Islam has not changed in any fundamental respect since its founding in the 7th century. It has simply been refined in its details and interpreted to govern *all* human action, regardless of race, region, or nation. Christianity and Judaism underwent changes that made them tolerant of secular, exo-religious values, such as freedom of speech. Men who saw no value in stagnation, who wished to exercise their minds and be free to act, waged a long and bloody conflict with religious and political authority in the West, and won. If the Church claimed it ruled men to save their immortal souls, men replied that their souls were not the Church's to save.

Islam cannot cede such an argument. There are no doctrinaire loopholes in the system. It is all-encompassing, and allows no exceptions to its rule. To be "saved" by Islam is to submit to it without reason and in every particular. Your "soul" is Allah's to save or to condemn.

Jihad Watch's article lists several attributes prevalent in technologically and economically advanced Western and Westernized nations (the latter including India and Japan), but which are largely absent in any given Islamic culture: an absence of personal responsibility, of innovation, of "devotion" to any idea or organization beyond family, tribe or clan, of equality of women and men in terms of politics and economics, of skilled labor, and of a "meritocracy." Included in the list are a belief in magic and an obsession with conspiracies (against tribes, against Islam, and so on), but these will not be discussed here.

The Jihad Watch article is correct and well-intentioned, but woefully lacking itself in explaining why the West has surpassed Islam. Without establishing the broader context of why and how innovation, "devotion," skilled labor and so on exist in the West but not in Muslim culture, the list seems wholly arbitrary. One could easily substitute "honesty," "diet" or "education" for any of the others, or simply add them to the list.

"Innovation," for example, requires not only the freedom to create and invent, but the *desire* to think. *Capitalism* fosters and rewards the freedom and the desire. Islam suffocates and punishes them. The article makes this odd statement about "meritocracy," which is likely a euphemism for capitalism.

> The West has thrived not only because they [sic] have learned to hold people responsible for their actions, but also they have learned to give out rewards based on individual achievement. Hence higher–performing individuals tend to be eventually in charge and reap the most rewards (in prestige, rank, money, etc.).

Who are "they" who are "giving out rewards" to individuals? And who are the "high-performing Individuals" who will eventually take charge and reap the most rewards? This could just as well be a description of a communist or fascist society, of the Soviet Union or Nazi Germany. Prestige, rank, and (legally looted) money are paramount values in collectivist societies, even in Islamic ones. If the author of the article is pro-capitalism, his choice of words is ill-considered.

Linked to the "meritocracy" issue, although the author treats it as a separate issue, is "personal responsibility," which he attributes solely to political leaders.

Muslim leaders often lie to or deceive their own people, to subordinates, or to allies in order to advance their own personal agendas. Remember that most Muslim countries are a patchwork of tribes who barely tolerate one another in the best of times. Loyalty to one's country as a whole is next to non-existent. So, the main objective of these leaders, whether at the top, middle or bottom, is to steal as much as they can, while they can, in order to enrich themselves and their families, clans or tribes—'national interest' be damned.

But personal responsibility is also a private, non-political characteristic, as well. One can take responsibility for an accomplishment as well as for an error in thinking or a disaster. Western politicians, however, are as notorious for lying to and deceiving their constituents as are their Muslim counterparts (the *modus operandi* of the current occupant of the White House). They are indemnified against lawsuits no matter how disastrous and destructive their policies are, and insulated from their consequences with hefty salaries and generous packages of fringe benefits (all paid for by productive, responsible taxpayers). If their policies produce the opposite of what they intend, they will blame external forces beyond their control or anyone's comprehension. They cultivate "patchworks" of special interests – lobbies, or "tribes, if you will – and will advocate and enact progressive laws, propose burdensome regulations, and append pork barrel programs to other bills that are in fundamental conflict with the "national interest," regardless of their oaths of office to uphold and defend the Constitution.

Barney Frank and Harry Reid are not shaking in their boots. There are never untoward repercussions for them – only for the electorate. They are no better than any Arab sheik, general, or dictator when it comes to venality and theft.

Again, the author of the article chose a poor example to demonstrate why the West differs from Islamic cultures. This is the trouble with purported conservative advocates of freedom, and that article exemplifies it: theirs is a disintegrated moral and political philosophy, akin to the asteroid belt that never coalesced into a planet. It is an itinerary of concretes that refer to ideas that just float in the space of their minds.

More to the point of how stuck in an insurmountable rut Islam is, Daniel Greenfield's article more closely examines the issue.

> Racial and religious doctrinal purity does not equal omnipotence. And Islamic expansionism is due to relearn the same lesson that World War II meted out to the aggressors. The Caliphate and Third Reich are the vision of maniacs and demagogues trying to turn back the clock to a mythical past. Building castles in the sand by a bloody shore.

> The obsessive petrodollar construction projects of Dubai have something of Albert Speer about them. Huge tasteless buildings constructed to show the grandeur of a regime, even while revealing its lack of taste and creativity. And its underlying insecurity. The Nazis', Communists' and now Muslims' obsession with constructing gargantuan inhuman structures reveal some of the insecurity behind the violence. Giant concrete and steel security blankets by vicious men terrified of their own mortality.

Built also to demonstrate an efficacy that is founded on the fallacy of force. Greenfield's thesis is that Islam must expand or perish. It cannot be content to rule over mere dime-a-dozen believers. It must conquer, loot, plunder, rape and murder. Raymond Ibrahim of the Middle East Forum features a story about just how necessary force and conquest are to the Islamic mind.

On the one hand, Islam causes Muslims to be incurious and indifferent to life-affirming values. How many Muslim critics have written approvingly about a Gilbert and Sullivan operetta, a Rachmaninoff concerto, an engineering marvel, or about an advance in medicine or technology? On the other hand, and at the same time, Islam encourages Muslims to be hostile to those values, hostile from an intractable envy, and envy that can morph into a desire to eradicate them.

Islam fosters cultural, political, and economic stagnation because individualism is an anathema to it. An absence of freedom of speech inculcates minds that lack any measure of intellectual vigor in any human action, whether in politics, science, or art. If one fears to say what is on one's mind, even to oneself, nothing will happen. One treads water in a brackish pond of the unassailable given. That is the condition of most Muslims, who are locked in a stasis of their own making. They are alive, but, for all practical purposes, they are dead. Their cognitive faculties have atrophied. They become interchangeable ciphers. (I always cite the analogy of The Borg from the TV series, *Star Trek: The Next Generation.*)

Their only assurance or guarantee that the universe is reliable and knowable is to submit to pointless rituals and to accept the word of their moral "superiors" (imams, mullahs). They become immune to reason. They are incapable of valuing anything beyond the concrete aspects of their creed; they develop a seething hostility and hatred for anyone or anything that contradicts their unchallenged, unquestioned assumptions. Woe to any Muslim who violates the arbitrary diktats of Mohammed. Thus the killings, stonings, hangings, and so on. They become super-sensitive to any criticism of their beliefs, because the criticism is not only a threat to them, but also because criticism implies a world-view that is possible beyond their warped metaphysics and epistemology. It is an existence they have surrendered. Muslims are not capable of starting anything like the American Revolution; the so-called "Arab Spring" is fundamentally a hankering for a friendlier despot.

Islam would indeed expire should it ever achieve the global caliphate its advocates boast is their end. Islam would act like a cancer; once it had debilitated and enveloped the host, it would perish with the host. That is because Islam is essentially a nihilist ideology. One can point to any Middle Eastern nation dominated by Islam and see a preview of a world governed by Islam – except that the ensuing and necessary poverty and misery would be global in nature, and not just regional. If there are skyscrapers in Dubai and some economic life in Egypt, it is only because a West exists that created those values. Emulation is not creativity. Like Soviet communism, it can only copy the achievements of the West, and poorly at that. If Islam denies men the right to think, to move, to challenge, to innovate, to risk, to live their own lives free from fear of retribution, then the reduction of men to thinking only about the next minute or next day, is all that can be achieved – or, universal destruction and a new dark age.

One of the virtues of George Orwell's dystopian novel, *Nineteen Eighty-Four*, is that, while it was written as a "prophetic satire," it contains such a plentitude of truisms and perceptive observations that it is taken as a blueprint for successful totalitarianism. The world of Winston Smith, however, is impossible in reality. That is one of the bones I have to pick with the novel. As a feasible political stasis, the totalitarian state described by Orwell would not survive. It would not be industrial, or productive, or self-sustaining. One doesn't choke off men's capacity to think and act and expect them to continue producing steel, or medicine, or art.

But there is one particular feature of it that stands out and which would guarantee the short-lived existence of such a political establishment.

Much is made of "Newspeak," the program devised by the totalitarians to stunt men's minds by reducing the number of approved and politically-correct concepts available to men in their vocabulary, and in particular to the ruling Inner and Outer Party members. Its purpose is to render impossible any hint of rebellion, betrayal, or resistance *within the Party*. Such is Orwell's respect for language that he even devotes an afterward to the subject. But if such a state were actually attained – with Party members communicating with each other by means of a deliberately emaciated lexicon of operative terms, they would be rendered helpless against the first men to reinvent the concepts. If all memory of standard concepts that we take for granted today was eradicated – nouns, verbs, adjectives, conjunctions, articles – and replaced with a suffocating, mind-stunting written and spoken jargon, no communication would be possible between the rulers and the ruled.

Likewise, Islam must adhere to the approved lexicon that appears in the *Koran* and *Hadith* (the alleged canonical "sayings" of Mohammad, much like Mao's *Little Red Book* of quotations), or perish. It cannot adopt new terms without admitting a flood of concepts alien to its intent which would simply adulterate and dissolve the doctrine. It cannot even attempt to redefine its most belligerent and aggressive terms without reducing its already primitive doctrine to certifiable gibberish and "speaking in tongues."

Any new terms must be *Western* terms, introduced to amend or qualify the brutish, criminal ones that characterize Islamic literature. Islam's purists – the sheiks, the imams, the mullahs – can be likened to the Orwell's Inner Party, which wields more power over rank-and-file Outer Party Muslims than it does over the infidels and dhimmis. They are the gimlet-eyed guardians of the Islamic lexicon as well as of the faith, for the purity of the faith depends wholly on the purity of its words. "It is written" is not merely a hubristic assertion of predestination; in Islamic metaphysics, Mohammad's words are as real and unalterable as a rock. That is another cause of Islam's viral stasis. And another reason why Islam cannot be reformed without killing it.

I agree with Greenfield that Islam must at some point disintegrate and self-destruct. But that may not happen until it has made too many inroads in a Western culture that denies its own exceptionalism, a culture that once upheld reason, individualism, and freedom as its distinctive and empowering virtues. Islam must first succeed in corrupting the spirit of its enemies before it rots itself. Islam is a parasite; it can make progress only by grace of the timidity of its adversaries and the mindless, obedient plain song of its billion-plus collect. It derives its strength from the weakness and cowardice and compromise of its enemies. If Islam succeeds in conquering the West, it can only die with it. The most rabid of its advocates know this. They are death worshippers. A Dark Age is the only cultural environment they will feel comfortable in.

Islam is otherwise impotent.

June 2011

The Murderous "Mind-Sets" of Mysticism

Ayn Rand identified and named the two species of anti-man, anti-life mystics that have largely governed man's history: the mystics of spirit, and the mystics of muscle.

It is rare that two prominent mystics appear on the world stage at the same time to deliver their ultimata: Pope Benedict XVI and President Mahmoud Ahmadinejad of Iran. Pope Benedict's appearance and utterances on September 23 passed almost unnoticed, while Ahmadinejad's appearance at Columbia University on September 24 garnered international headlines.

Columbia University's invitation to Ahmadinejad to speak to an audience of students, faculty and the public provoked a firestorm of opposition, chiefly from those who challenged the propriety of extending the courtesy to a dictator who not only imprisons, murders and brutalizes people in his own country, but whose government funds international terrorism and whose agents are helping to kill Americans in Iraq.

Aside from the impropriety of inviting a self-proclaimed *enemy* to speak anywhere in this country, never mind at a noted university, there is the question of what President Lee C. Bollinger of Columbia thought he could accomplish by the invitation. He cited the prerogative of making such an invitation in the name of "free speech."

Since the Press Law of Iran cited by Bollinger forbids criticism of the government in any form whatsoever, that is, forbids freedom of speech, why extend the right to a dictator responsible for the censorship and repression? Is the right to free speech extended to convicted criminals? By any objective standard, for having committed capital crimes, have they not forfeited the right to freedom of speech? Is not that forfeiture a part of their punishment and incarceration?

In defending his decision to invite Ahmadinejad, Bollinger said during his opening remarks at the event that "this is the right thing to do and, indeed, it is required by existing norms of free speech...."

What are those norms? Bollinger did not elaborate. Do those norms include welcoming a monster who, at his Nuremberg-like rallies in Tehran, regularly calls the U.S. the "Great Satan" and predicts and prays for its destruction at his hand?

One also must wonder what he believed he could accomplish by accusing Ahmadinejad of exhibiting "all the signs of a petty and cruel dictator," and by reading from a list of crimes committed by the dictator. Did he expect Ahmadinejad to acknowledge the truth of Bollinger's damnation, suffer an incapacitating guilt attack, then wreathe and weep in heart-wrenching contrition? What was the point? If he was hoping for a "robust debate" of his charges against Ahmadinejad, the robustness of the "confrontation" was an eminently one-sided one. The vulpine Ahmadinejad demonstrated agility in evasive sophistry matched only by Hillary Clinton when cornered by facts and fault.

Bollinger's list of charges against Ahmadinejad included the jailing and execution of Iranians for demanding freedom of speech, in addition to denying the Holocaust, advocating the destruction of Israel, funding terrorism, providing men and weapons to fight Americans in Iraq, and denying that Iran is working to develop a nuclear bomb.

Ahmadinejad slithered around every one of those charges and every one of the pointed questions put to him by members of the audience. Reading a transcript of his address, there is in it not a single direct answer to any one of Bollinger's charges or an honest answer to any of the audience's questions.

Bollinger expressed his subtle estimate of Ahmadinejad during his rationalization of why the dictator should be allowed to speak:

> "It is consistent with the idea that one should know thine enemies, to have the intellectual and emotional courage to confront the mind of evil and to prepare ourselves to act with the right temperament."

But if the enemy is already known, and if one knows that his mind is evil (or what Bollinger characterized as Ahmadinejad's "fanatical mindset"), why "confront" it in debate? Did we debate with Hitler of Nazi Germany or Tojo of Imperial Japan the rightness or wrongness of their aggression and atrocities?

Bollinger cautioned against "the very natural but often counter-productive impulses that lead us to retreat from engagement with ideas we dislike and fear."

But Ahmadinejad has no idea but one: brute force. He does not wish to "engage" with ideas he dislikes and fears and which do not conform to his intrinsicist universe of Islam. Ideas emanate from minds, and it is minds he wishes to bypass and ultimately subdue or destroy – which is the leitmotif of Islam. He dismissed Bollinger's moral indignation as irrelevant, almost comical.

Bollinger also revealed himself as an intrinsicist. His premise was that knowledge of the "good" was somehow an innate resident of Ahmadinejad's mind as a repressed operative, and that what he wished to "discourse" with Ahmadinejad was why the dictator did not acknowledge it.

Ahmadinejad did not acknowledge it. He has his own set of intrinsic values, all subsumed under Islamic theology. He called Bollinger's charges "insulting."

Ahmadinejad's address was not so much a speech or a lecture as a sermon, and he began it, appropriately enough, with an invocation. "In the name of God, the compassionate, the merciful....Oh, God, hasten the arrival of Imam al-Mahdi and grant him good health and victory and make us his followers and those to attest to his rightfulness...."

Perhaps it was lost on or forgotten by Bollinger and the audience, not to mention the press, that Ahmadinejad regards himself as the next "Mahdi," the expected spiritual and temporal leader of Muslims, and in that role he is preparing the way for the return of the Hidden or Twelfth Imam by laying the groundwork for Armageddon or the Apocalypse. The joke was on Bollinger and the audience; the Mahdi *had* arrived, and he was Ahmadinejad.

Ahmadinejad's sermon was such a vile and bizarre *soufflé* of Koranic references, prattlings about science, scholars, light and "realities," oblique insinuations of the crimes of American "imperialism" past and present, commiserations about the plight of the Palestinians, and querulous babblings about the ill-treatment of Iran, that it would be fruitless to try to summarize it all here. Its general tone was a combination of an appeal to pity and an appeal to guilt.

(Ahmadinejad's speech at the U.N. was even more bizarre. He lectured the General Assembly almost exclusively on the virtues of the Hidden Imam. But then, the U.N. is a bizarrely immoral, anti-U.S. institution anyway, which the U.S sanctions with its membership.)

If one wanted proof of Ahmadinejad's mystical roots and fundamental irrationality, one statement of his at Columbia stands out:

> "Realities of the world are not limited to physical realities and the materials, [they are] just a shadow of supreme reality. And physical creation is just one of the stories of the creation of the world."

Ahmadinejad has read his Koran *and* his Kant. Both Bollinger and his "guest" are intrinsicists, but Ahmadinejad harbors a strong streak of whim-worshipping subjectivism, as well, against which Bollinger's anger was impotent. He ended his rant with, "We are a peaceful, loving nation. We love all nations."

He loves them enough to either conquer them or destroy them, just as Hitler loved Europe and Japan loved Asia.

One does not invite killers to a civilized venue to merely scold them for their crimes. One arrests them, or shoots them, or eradicates their murderous governments. Ahmadinejad in this instance was the *enemy* and should have been denied entry into this country. Instead, both Bollinger and the U.S., in the names of "fairness" and diplomatic protocol, allowed him to come here to take advantage of propaganda platforms, and he left "victorious and in good health."

It was not Allah or God who was merciful and compassionate and who answered Ahmadinejad's prayers. It was the State Department and the President of Columbia University. It is such mercy and compassion that will be the death of us.

Pope Benedict's pronouncements on Sunday the 23rd were a kind of warm-up act to Ahmadinejad's. In his own sermons, according to *The Scotsman* of the 24th, under the headline, "Pope urges rich to turn from Satan and help the poor," he "denounced what he called the world's 'profit mind-set'…warning that money can turn people into 'blind egoists' as he urged the wealthy to share their riches with the poor.

> "Benedict said life was about making choices between good and bad, between altruism and egoism, honesty and dishonesty….Ultimately, he said, it was about making the choice between God and Satan."

Yes, life is about making choices, and knowing that those choices enable one to live – if one's purpose is to live. If one makes the wrong choices, one suffers or dies. Benedict has those choices inverted, however. If one chose between good and bad by his criteria, one would indeed suffer or die. It requires honesty to assert that one owns one's own life, and that one lives selfishly. It requires dishonesty to profess otherwise.

> "…When the mind-set of sharing and solidarity prevails, you can correct your course and change it to a sustainable and equal development," said Benedict.

> "The pope called for a 'conversion' of economic goods," said *The Scotsman* article. "'Rather than using them for self-interest, we should also think about the needs of the poor, imitating Christ,' he said."

Once a National Socialist, always a National Socialist. There's a "mind-set" for you.

One might innocently pose these questions to Benedict: If the rich and the middle class heeded his altruistic homilies, and shared their wealth with the poor – then what? Who or what would generate more wealth to give away? Would not such a mass transfer of wealth trigger an economic collapse, and impoverish everyone? Would not everyone then be literally staring starvation and death in the face?

Aye, there's the rub! That is the secret, unexpressed mutual goal of both Ahmadinejad and Pope Benedict. They are humanitarians, "lovers" of mankind, mystics of muscle and mind.

Rand had personal names for them: Attila and the Witch Doctor.

September 2007

Islam the Alien

For me, most science fiction stories have a credibility problem. But the one branch of it whose premise I have always rejected is that alien life could be both malevolent and technologically advanced enough to embark on interstellar conquests. Films such as *Predator* and *Independence Day* – just two of the more popular instances of the genre among many – portray aliens stalking man as a species of game or subjugating or extinguishing him. The premise that projects the possibility of these creatures is that a preeminently hostile, anti-life-form could somehow apply reason to create spaceships and sophisticated weaponry.

However, life-forms so malevolent would never rise from the rank swamps that bred them to go zipping around star systems and blasting planets to atoms. Malevolence is not a progenitor of innovation or creation. It is fundamentally a parasite and can thrive only on a passive or willing host. Reason is not an attribute or a handmaiden of evil. Evil in fact can only exploit the products of reason, but never originate them. Evil men or evil aliens may exhibit *intelligence*, but not reason. They can exploit what reason has caused to exist, but never bring it into existence.

Ugly predators and slimy aliens that can invent cloaking devices and disintegrating rays are possible in imagination only because of a fantastic, and possibly even fatal, fallacy. Their creators – and their fans – assume that reason is not the natural antithesis and enemy of anti-reason, but a morally neutral faculty that can ally itself with anti-reason in campaigns of conquest and death.

Not so coincidentally, the fallacy also explains the left's hostility to freedom and capitalism. Capitalists, they say, have the freedom to employ reason to create things, and then use their profits to establish power and enslave everyone.

Sharks, rattlesnakes, Komodo dragons, wolves, and other predators are not inherently evil. They do what nature has programmed them to do, without any choice in their struggles for existence. No moral decisions are involved in their actions. Their values are predetermined. They lack the attribute of volition, that is, the capacity to think or not to think, to choose what will sustain and improve their lives and what will not.

A malevolent intelligence is not a contraction in terms. Else how to explain all the real and fictional villains in history and literature, from Hitler to Professor Moriarty, from Attila the Hun to Ellsworth Toohey? Or Iran's Mahmoud Ahmadinejad and his threatened nuclear weapons? But a malevolent adherent to reason, like the aliens in *Predator* and

Independence Day, is a psychological, metaphysical and philosophical contradiction. In nature, the teleology of such alien creatures is impossible.

A malevolent intelligence may succeed in finding comfort in a social and material environment created by reason, and be able to exploit its victims' innocence, foolishness, or ignorance. But without reason having created such a world, it would remain a miserable prisoner in the dank, fetid jungle it was born in, never able to conceive of anything better, unable by its nature to look up at the stars, content with its surroundings, and concerned only with its next meal. Thomas Hobbes' notion of man at war is equally and more realistically applicable to the actual existence of would-be predator space aliens in their basic mode: solitary, poor, nasty, brutish, and short.

Which leads me to Islam.

Islam is a malevolent, ideational predator bent on conquest. It demands conversion, submission, or death. Left to its own devices, Islam would have remained contained by and confined to its own impotence whence it came, the Mideast, in Saudi Arabia. It would be a bubonic rat that squeaked but which would otherwise be quarantined by its own irrationality, and by reason.

But what has given Islam its purported potency to wreck havoc in the world? It is a philosophy burdened with the same fallacy that allows science fiction writers to believe that reason can ally with anti-reason and act of its own accord. In past columns I have likened Islam to a drooling beast, to the Borg, to a viral disease, and to other entities closed to reason, proof against freedom, and dedicated to destruction for destruction's sake.

Pragmatic policies in the West allowed the nomadic, primitive Saudis and other tribalists to nationalize the oil which Western technology discovered and developed in the barren wastes over which they had been butchering each other and other tribes for millennia. Environmentalist policies that prohibit oil drilling allow smug tribalists to make extortion a practical policy. Pragmatic policies allowed Muslims to immigrate to semi-free, semi-rational cultures and proceed to complete the sabotaging disease of irrationality. Pragmatism sired moral and cultural relativism that forbids moral judgment of Islam's barbarism and its incipient, cradle-to-grave psychosis. Appropriating the mantle of "religious freedom" – call it a "cloaking device," if you will – and exploiting the foolishness and irrationality of their enemies, Islamic activists in three-piece suits and armed with unlimited funds work obsessively to erase freedom for all but Muslims.

Pragmatism fosters the growth of a police state whose managers and minions, in the name of political correctness and non-discrimination, will not identify Islam as a predatory ideology (that would be evidence of "Islamophobia," and "offensive"), and proceed to subject and inure a country's citizens to the invasive ministrations of arbitrary searches, seizures, and incarceration on the chance that they might catch a bomber whose motives will not be linked to Islam. Their policy, designed to not offend Muslims but all non-Muslims, is to hope to find a scimitar in an infinite haystack. The Department of Homeland Security is headed by a multiculturalist friendly to Islam, while the TSA is staffed by tens of thousands of non-entities empowered to grope, violate, molest, rob, and hold judgment over private citizens in the name of "safety."

The anti-profiling policies of the DHS and TSA are anti-reason, and anti-Aristotelian, and as "alien" as the ends of a Predator or shapeless alien piloting five-mile-wide spaceships.

Islam is such a unique, unprecedented peril that one ignores it at one's own peril. There is the double peril of Obama, Pelosi, et al. (and the generations of collectivist thought behind them) wanting to "transform" the country into a secular State of Servitude (no pun intended), and of Islam, whose spokesmen are at work insinuating its brand of totalitarianism into the country via "religious freedom," but whose purpose is also to "transform" the country into another kind of State of Servitude. In this teleological end Islamists have a willing ally, the secular totalitarians.

Saul Alinsky, meet Sheikh Ahmad Gad of the Muslim Brotherhood, another malevolent intelligence.

Islam is a radically different matter. None of the other religious groups in America – whether they are composed largely of immigrants or of tenth generation blacks or whites or Asians or Eskimos – expects the other creeds to defer to it. Muslims and Islam, however, expect everyone to defer to Islam. Islam is an enemy of individualism. Islam is imbued with a code of conduct that is fundamentally barbaric and concrete-bound and too often murderous. Sharia is not just a primitive system of adjudication; it is also, and inherently, political. It does not recognize the world beyond that insular system, except as something to assimilate into its system, or to erase.

The corrupting norms of multiculturalism have vastly aided Muslims in their not having to knuckle under secular law and having to stop murdering wayward daughters and wives and sons who become apostates. Furthermore, feminists, liberals, leftists in and out of academia ignore the outrages committed by Muslims in the name of Islam – the continuing rapes of 'infidel" women in Europe and the Mideast by Muslims, the stonings, hangings, and executions of men and women who flout Islamic rules, the persecution and murders of Christians, Jews, Hindus in the name of Islam, and so on – because they recognize Islam as a bird of the same feather – a totalitarian system that shares similar premises, methods, and ends. Criticism of rival totalitarians might inadvertently lead to criticism of their own anti-reason and anti-life policies. Call the phenomenon a Collectivist-Islamic Non-Aggression Pact.

Predatory "aliens" need not come from outer space. There are two species of them right here on earth, both exercising their malevolent intelligences to advance their dual agendas of conquest, slavery, and destruction. They are merely rivals, and not antipodes of each other.

As Gilliatt did in Victor Hugo's compelling novel, *Toilers of the Sea*, as he was being enveloped by an octopus's arms, and as the creature's flesh-tearing beak struggled to strike him, we need to free ourselves from Islamic jihad not by cutting off its arms: but its head. Only reason and rationality can accomplish that end. That done, the arms will go limp and release us to pursue our life-affirming values in freedom without peril or hindrance. It is the ideology that must be damned, renounced, repudiated, and defeated, with no apologies or regrets, and not its surface manifestations.

Then we will have the time to turn our attention to performing the same surgery on the secular totalitarian ideology that also seeks to vanquish this country.

July 2011

PBS airs "Islam for Dhimmis"

A spell of insomnia saw me up early Wednesday morning (April 25). I poured a glass of milk and tried to read Taine's "Introduction to the History of English Literature." But my mind was too restless to concentrate, so I switched on the television to see what anyone else up at so ungodly an hour would be watching, aside from Jay Leno, "infomercials," or national news. I would settle for anything that would induce drowsiness.

Lo and behold, what did I encounter at 3:05 a.m. on Channel 15, the local Public Broadcasting System station out of Norfolk, but propaganda for Islam. I have not been able to learn the actual name of the program. Several calls to the station's program director asking for its name have not been returned. In the newspaper TV listings, a block of hours from 2 a.m. to 4 a.m. was marked simply "Varied Programs." Not "various"? But, never mind.

However, if it is to have a name, it should be dubbed either "Islam for Real Dummies" or "Islam for Dhimmis." Billed certainly as a "documentary," it left out a great mass of very crucial documents, leaving one with the question in one's mind: If Islam is such a mellow, benign creed, how could anyone hold a brief on it? It was such a solemn yet saccharine encomium it could just as well have been a promotion for the Rotary Club or the Knights of Columbus.

But, my tax dollars were at work, shilling for Mohammad.

This is the kind of "educational" film doubtless shown to gullible, impressionable, ignorant teenagers in high schools, in the same rank as films shown them about environmentalism, recycling, tolerance, sex, global warming, and "democracy." Perhaps it is even shown in middle or grade schools, our Comprachico-trained public school authorities having a policy of brainwashing children as early as possible.

Now, I had not seen such a "puff piece" (thanks to Richard Brinsley Sheridan's *The Critic* for that term) since Michael Moore's last effort at disinformation and Al Gore's "An Inconvenient Truth," so "Islam for Dhimmis" was a special experience. I will not recount everything that was in the film, but focus on some highlights.

One image sticks in my mind, that of a comely young Muslim woman, appropriately attired in an immaculately white hair-and-neck-hiding scarf, being interviewed about the Islamic notion of charity. "If you can't give someone money, then Mohammad says you should reward him with a smile. Mohammad is such a wonderful role model!" She said it with her best Moonie smile, as well. That whole segment of the half-hour program was devoted to the Fourth Pillar of Islam, of giving alms to the poor as a matter of duty and as "purification" of one's wealth. (I immediately thought of Bill Gates and Warren Buffet, and the penance they haven't chosen to perform with their wealth.)

Smile? No mention was made anywhere in the program of all the smiles hidden by the ski masks worn by the troops of Hezbollah or Hamas or by the murderers of Nick Berg, Daniel Pearl, or of any other "infidel" Westerner similarly subjected to such compassion.

Another image that sticks in my mind is the footage of Hajj pilgrims thronging by the tens of thousands around the Kaaba in Mecca, a veritable sea of wild-eyed manqués who hope to hike around the place seven times and press their lips to the Black Stone, and by kissing it, add their own sins to its likely unsanitary surface. No footage, however, was shown of the usual stampedes of the faithful that result in hundreds of them being crushed to death as surely as if the Black Stone fell on them from the sky, leaving behind mountains of empty sandals. So much for the Fifth Pillar of Islam.

The program's take on the early history of Islam was interesting in that it was a model of how to gloss over historical facts. After Mohammad captured Mecca and died shortly thereafter, his followers spread the faith throughout the Middle East, Africa, and into parts of southern Europe – by the sword. In the program, however, this was not called "conquest" by force of arms and threat of annihilation. Islam's history was presented in so slick a manner that an uncritical mind would have gone away thinking that it was a peaceful spread of the creed, involving no slaughters, mayhem, destruction, or the enslavement of whole populations.

It was left to the dhimmi mind to infer that the success of Allah's gospel was the work of just hard-working imams and mullahs and Sufis preaching the Word in pagan lands, just like St. Patrick in Ireland. It implied that the conquerors respected the religions of the populations they subdued, and all was well. There was no mention of the fact that those populations the Islamists permitted to keep their religions, were obliged to pay *jizya*, protection money that was a sign of submission and dhimmitude, a condition of "coexistence" which meant little more than dhimmis getting the hell out of the way of any Muslim.

The narrator did not broach the subject that Islam could spread only because the final collapse of Greco-Roman civilization created a political/military vacuum that allowed Islam to sweep through the known world in the south and the Huns and Visigoths to sweep down from the north, probably because it was history that did not fit the thesis.

Another segment on "colonialism" was equally interesting. For some strange, unexplained reason, Islam declined in the 19th century, allowing Western powers to colonize great portions of the expiring semi-caliphate of Islam, overrunning North Africa, the Middle East, and as far away as Indonesia. There was a peculiar focus on British, French, and Dutch colonialism, complete with old footage of soldiers dispersing mobs of presumably Muslims with guns, bayonets and swords. In the late 19th century, according to the program, "resentment" over Islam's decline and the power of the West grew. I am supposing that was the program producer's way of cocking a snook at Britain, France and the Netherlands, which now have the most contentious, unassimilated Muslim populations.

That "resentment" covers a lot of territory not even hinted at in the program, including fatwas, jihads, and anti-Semitism. "Resentment" was probably the softest term the program's scriptwriter could come up with and have approved by his Islamic script consultants to stand in for "hatred," that is, for hatred of the West for being the West and for being superior, as well.

Interestingly, not once was the role of oil brought up during the program. The footage of the 1930's and 1940's suddenly depicted Arab emirs and princes debouching from airplanes and taking part in international conferences, with no explanation of how or why tribal chieftains could suddenly do these things. No mention was made of all the expropriated, Western developed oil fields in the Mideast that Western governments neglected to defend for their owners (and whose owners capitulated and "cooperated" with the expropriations to form such bastard entities as ARAMCO). All those skinny Bedouin emirs and princes grew very fat; look at the members of the House of Saud today.

In explaining the character and content of Islam, the narrator said that Islam recognizes only one God (Allah), and that Mohammad is his prophet. He did not go on to point out one major implication of that belief, to wit, that if Mohammad is not any other creed's prophet, then it is a false creed and consequently a legitimate target for repression and ultimate elimination by Islam. This theological Catch-22 is blatantly obvious, yet it is astounding that it is not grasped by most who comment on Islam (including Pope Benedict). It is a central tenet of Islam; remove it, or demote Mohammad to just one of a gaggle of Muslim prophets, and Islam would implode as a religious/political ideology.

(Similarly, Jesus Christ was not the only religious "savior" of his time to be crucified by the Romans; imagine the consequences throughout Christianity if that icon were shattered, as well. How many candidates for the role of "son of God" were there originally? Did the authors of the Bible draw up a short list, or hold an "American Idol" style talent contest to judge who was the most pacific?)

This, neither the Islamic "extremists" nor the "moderates" will or can allow to happen. No one but an unbeliever or an apostate would propose the idea, because doing so would immediately earn him a fatwa or death sentence. (Call it the Muslim "Wanted: Dead or Alive" bulletin board.). Re Salman Rushdie, Wafa Sultan, Oriana Fallaci, Ayaan Hirsi Ali, Steve Emerson, and others. The roll call of those with the intellectual honesty and courage to excoriate Islam grows daily, but it is not given much press.

Also mentioned by the narrator with great deference in this segment was the fact that neither humans nor animals are permitted representation in Islamic art. This, he and some imam explained, is to discourage icons and to encourage the perception of Allah and Mohammad as "abstractions." The narrator spoke dozens of words about the beauty of Islamic architecture and the grace of Islamic calligraphy, but did not once allude to the Danish cartoons and the uproar by thousands of "tolerant" and "compassionate" Muslims calling for the cartoonists' deaths.

In all the program, no breath of suggestion was made about: the bestial strictures of Sharia law, honor killings, fatwas on apostates and defamers of Islam, beheadings, the regular slaughter of infidels, the jihad against the West, 9/11, the London, Madrid and Bali bombings – all that and more credited to Islam, about Islam, in Islam's name.

The end credits were not surprising. The half-hour program was made possible by "The Royal Embassy of Saudi Arabia," "The Government of Kuwait," and "The Islamic Center," and was produced by Delphi Productions. The credits rolled down so quickly I may have missed a few other sponsor names.

I do not know if "Islam for Dhimmis" was ever aired during prime time and if this was just a rerun to fill a dead time slot in the wee hours. If my queries to WHRO Channel 15 are ever answered, I will report what is told me. It would be interesting, however, to learn who funded the production of this instance of catholic cosmetology and vetted the final cut. Probably the usual suspects, here and abroad.

It would be pointless to protest the use of my tax dollars to advance a religious doctrine by a government-funded entity such as PBS, especially a doctrine so antithetical to the principles of freedom on which this country was founded. The high Pooh-Bahs of the Corporation for Public Broadcasting, like their counterparts in the BBC, would dismiss such a protest with scorn. PBS broadcasts so many programs that are antithetical that it would be churlish to upbraid it over this program alone. As have the private broadcasters – ABC, CBS, NBC, CNN, etc. – it has bought into the collectivist/altruist ideological axis without the least sign of discrimination or fastidiousness, without the least regard for its totalitarian potential. All that is protected by the sacred cow of "public service."

Given the ongoing Islamist jihad against the West, the airing of "Islam for Dhimmis" is an unforgivable public "disservice," and for that offense alone, PBS should be defunded and abolished.

April 2007

Islamic Goals

Reader: Reflect on these quotations:

Omar Ahmad, the founder of the Council of American-Islamic Relations (CAIR), said in a controversial interview:

> *"Islam isn't in America to be equal to any other religions, but to become dominant. The Koran, the Muslim book of scripture, should be the highest authority in America, and Islam the only accepted religion unearth."*

And, a quotation from the manifesto of The Muslim Brotherhood, by Mohamed Akram, May 19, 1991

> *"Eliminating and destroying Western civilization from within and 'sabotaging' its miserable house so that it is eliminated and God's religion is made victorious over all other religions."*

Enough said? Clear enough. Plain enough? If not, then here it is from the horse's mouth. Or Mohammad's. Supposedly. This is from a page from Bridgette Gabriel's *Act for America* blog site.

<u>61:9</u> *"...that He (Muhammad) may make it **conqueror of all religion** however much idolaters may be averse"* + <u>**48:28**</u> *"...to proclaim it over all religion"* + <u>9:33</u> *"...prevail over all religions"* <u>**8:39**</u> + <u>2:193</u> *"...and religion should be **only for Allah**"* + <u>3:189</u> *"And Allah's is the kingdom of the heavens and the earth...."*

ISLAM WILL CONQUER & DOMINATE THE WORLD

December 2012

The *"Smashers of Everything"*

In 1781, the year of America's decisive victory over Britain at Yorktown, there appeared in Europe a book of philosophy called *The Critique of Pure Reason.* When he read it, a friend of its author wailed and called his colleague "the smasher of everything." *The Critique* did not lay the groundwork for the attack on America on September 11, 2001; that act's perpetrators were applying the fundamental tenets of a creed founded in the 7th century. What that book did, aside from heralding a sustained, wholesale repudiation of reason and the pro-man Age of Enlightenment, was ultimately sanction that creed and disarm America. The author hijacked the term *reason* in order to destroy reason, just as Islamic militants hijacked the products of reason to destroy their symbols. His entire career was devoted to rescuing Christianity from the mortal influence of reason; his purpose, therefore, differed in no instance from the purpose of the plane hijackers and their superiors, which is to save Islam by becoming "smashers of everything" Western.

The author's name is Immanuel Kant. He was a professor of logic and metaphysics at a university in authoritarian Prussia. He taught that man can know nothing, and that things could be and not be at the same time. His intellectual descendents have a near-monopoly on the teaching of philosophy in politically correct American universities.

This writer, a novelist, was faced with the problem of how to tie the events of September 11th with his magnum opus, *Sparrowhawk,* without at the same time seeming to promote the book for purposes other than edification. From a literary standpoint, the chasm between our own time and the 18th century, when Kant thrived, seems vast and unbridgeable, separated from our interrogatory quest not only by the magnificent benevolence, progress, and confidence of the 19th century all that by grace of reason, but by our ignorance of both centuries. The contrasts between the politics, science, art, and Enlightenment philosophy of that era, and what passes for culture and enlightenment in our own, are violent and, at first glance, incomprehensible. Yet, the contrasts and their causes can be grasped by a mind willing to address the task, provided it employs the faculty of reason, man's only tool of survival. Anyone willing to accept that task is advised to adopt the motto of a fictional 20th century detective, who specialized in solving moral paradoxes: "Nothing that is observable in reality is exempt from rational scrutiny." Then the fundamental causes of the events of September 11 will come into sharp, merciless focus.

Sparrowhawk: Book One , Jack Frake, as well as subsequent titles in this series of historical novels, is about men who adopted that motto without ever giving it formal expression. Like its successor titles, which deal with other characters confronted with the same conflicts, Book One dramatizes the spirit of America by following, in word and deed, the infancy and development of a rational epistemology in the person of Jack Frake between the ages of ten and fifteen. Jack, like other men whose minds and spirits have not been corrupted, cowed, or crippled by doubt, fear, or education, is not concerned with the metaphysics of his own existence or that of the universe. He knows that he exists, and that the universe exists. They are irreducible primaries.

In the novel, Jack's concern is with his place in the world and his relationship to other men; that is, with morality and politics. The question of his place requires, for him, but a brief query: He existed, and was responsible for his own being and happiness. Every breath, every movement of his limbs, every act of thought, was caused by him and by him alone, for his own sake. By what right, then, he asks, do other men claim to have a divine or temporal interest in or power over him? None, he concludes. No one – not George II, not Robert Walpole, not Parliament, not God – had a right to one moment or one particle of the marvelous fact of his own existence. In this way, he contradicts the metaphysics of those who lived for and by others through guile, fraud, or force. And so, in an age prepared by Newton and Locke, and celebrated by Handel, Vivaldi, and later by Mozart, Jack becomes an outlaw in mid-18th century England.

America is such an outlaw, in the eyes of the chronically envious, such as Europe, in the eyes of dedicated, obsessive nihilists, such as the men who hurled planeloads of men, women, and children into the symbols of its outlawry, the World Trade Center and the Pentagon. It is an outlaw in the sense that America contradicts every tenet of the multifarious ethics that men exist solely for the state, for the collective, or for some Supreme Being. The World Trade Center was a symbol of man's successful living on earth; the Pentagon, of the successful defense of his life. In the eyes of our enemies, however, these symbols were as offensive as the sight of a leper, as threatening as a poisonous snake. They were metaphysical facts which their creed commanded them to wound, maim, or destroy. America is to them the "Great Satan," and these were the badges of its pride and efficacy.

The Founders of this country, together with their intellectual ancestors, John Locke and Aristotle, were responsible for those symbols. (Oh, yes, our Founders were intellectuals who performed a task since abandoned by most modern intellectuals, that of protecting this country from sabotage by Kant's fifth column subversives in our universities.) And when these symbols were attacked, so were the Declaration of Independence, the Constitution, capitalism, and life, liberty and the pursuit of happiness. It was an act of war, a war whose end is to end America, and to replace it with a static, suffocating nothingness – if "nothing" in this sense can be defined as a huddling collection of anonymous sub-humans whose miserable existence is sustained by and dependent on unthinking allegiance to God, Allah, or some form of dictatorship or totalitarianism – allegiance to anything but themselves as proudly free and unconquerably rational men.

The Founders went to great lengths to separate church from state. In this country, liberty's enemies preach an end similar to that of Islam's, or to that of secular totalitarians, which is to repeal that separation by Constitutional means or foul; I refer the reader to Jerry Falwell's and Pat Robertson's vicious remarks in the aftermath of the attack, and to recent, ill-disguised assaults on the Second Amendment by politicians and the courts.

The Founders were Christian Deists, who believed that God had distanced Himself from the affairs of men; indeed, from interference anywhere in the universe. (This was a view of God and man, a consequence of the Enlightenment, so feared by Kant.) They were painfully conscious of the effects and dangers of a state church, which existed then in England, France and in other European countries, and sought to eradicate this "tyranny over the mind of man" by separating state from church. Their reasoning was that since the state existed to protect an individual's rights, what the individual did to preserve his own soul was both his natural right and his business.

No such benevolent breach is possible in Islam. In Islamic philosophy, Allah and the state are fundamentally inseparable. An encyclopedia description of Islam is "the religion of which Mohammed was the prophet, the word signifying submission to the will of God." It is all or nothing for the individual: his choice is complete and unquestioning submission to Allah and his will, or the eternal status of "loser" in the eyes of Allah and the Muslim collective. Allah is the source of all law, civil and religious; Allah is universal and all-encompassing. This is why our politics has never successfully dealt with Muslim regimes. Our policymakers cannot credibly or effectively argue against the contradictions in Muslim "universal law" (never mind those present in Christian dogma) when they are the clueless heirs of Kant's dictum, transmitted by 19th and 20th century philosophers in a variety of forms in our universities, to "Act as if the maxim from which you act were to become through your will a universal law of nature" (from *The Fundamental Principles of the Metaphysics of Ethics*, 1785).

By Islamic precepts, all Christians, agnostics, atheists and others not of the Muslim faith are unbelievers and infidels, and, by extension of Allah's will, damned and dispensable. The creatures who ploughed into the World Trade Center and the Pentagon willed their own destruction and the deaths of their victims in the name of a "higher duty," one which, in all but name, can be classified as a Kantian "categorical imperative." Hatred is based on fear, and these automatons hated America for its steady erosion of a stagnant, life- and mind-stifling, undemanding credo, one in which self-loathing and self-sacrifice are supreme virtues. They achieved their maxim: death and destruction of the good for being the good, good being that which they could never achieve or be in life.

"The struggle against terrorism is ultimately a struggle of ideas, which can be dealt with only by intellectual and philosophical means," wrote Dr. Leonard Peikoff, foremost authority on Objectivism, the thoroughly, top-to-bottom pro-reason philosophy of Ayn Rand, after Black Tuesday on the requirements for defeating terrorism and the crucial necessity of persuading America to abandon its own suicidal policies. The Founders did not have the advantage of such a philosophy; they accomplished the best possible politics with what they inherited from the Enlightenment. We owe them a debt of gratitude.

But Americans must pick up where they left off, if they are to preserve themselves and this country, Western civilization, and all the glorious things possible to it and us. They should not mistake their nihilist enemies for "misguided idealists"; those enemies have marked us for extinction, and the notion that we are the objects of such malign "idealism" ought to be as outrageously repellent to them as it is to this writer, and send them running for their weapons like the Minutemen of old. Nor should they underestimate the scale of warfare that lies ahead; the enormity of the conflict surpasses that which caused the American Revolution.

From the beginning, one of my primary goals in Sparrowhawk was to dramatize what was required of men to accomplish not only political freedom from tyrants, but intellectual and psychological independence from any need of them. Free men, after all, are their own rulers. In that sense, Jack Frake and his brothers-in-spirit throughout Sparrowhawk will, I hope, serve as models of the kinds of men Americans might and ought to be. Then, perhaps, they will acquire the confidence and ability to fight and defeat the "smashers of everything," those beyond our shores, and those who assault us in our schools and universities, as well as in the culture at large.

September 2001

Note the similarity in design between the basic Obama logo above and that of Bill Ayers' Weather Underground above, to the left of the Palestine logo at the end of the second row.

The Current Administration

Obama's Emerging Enabling Act

Long, long ago, in a world far, far away, philosopher and cultural critic George Santayana in 1905 noted that "Those who cannot remember the past are condemned to repeat it."*

Have Americans learned from history? Have they any core knowledge of the past from which to draw wisdom, conclusions, and rational guidance? To judge by the record of the last half century – no. Perhaps a more pertinent question might be: Do they know history? Most

Americans are feeble on their own history, having never encountered much of it except for the Howard Ziinn- or Bill Ayers- style of history, or the multiculturalist brand, never mind world history or ancient history. They have been dumbed down and rendered ignorant of their own past. The Punic Wars? The Gates of Vienna? The Council of Nicaea? *Kristallnacht?*

These events may as well have occurred on a distant planet. Our educational establishment, at great taxpayer and personal cost, has seen to it that most Americans have been enfeebled from K1 up through college commencement, and has performed a pretty thorough and effective job of it. I've done enough booksignings to observe that more than one American has had a Jay Leno "man in the street" moment. Who crossed the Delaware? Lincoln. Who is Joe Biden? Isn't he a quarterback for the New England Patriots? Sharia Law? Wasn't she one of the Dixie Chicks? One can only blink in discreet and astonished trepidation.

The "Enablers" in the title of my previous post got me thinking about Adolf Hitler's Enabling Act of 1933. Its formal name was the Law to Remedy the Distress of the People and the Nation. This was a sweeping, across-the-board repudiation and nullification of what few liberties Germans had in the expiring Weimar Republic, a single, all-encompassing piece of legislation that ushered in the rule of men who subsequently buried the rule of law. Hitler demanded its passage. It would give him unobstructed and unprecedented power to impose his vision of Germany on the country.

Many Germans were enamored of that vision. It comported nicely with their shared sense of victimhood. He was their messiah. He had all the answers. He would do something to get them out of their economic rut, to restore the country's collective self-esteem, and resurrect Germany as a Teutonic power to be reckoned with.

The Act received overwhelming approval by the Reichstag, or the parliament, in March that year. And in approving it, it voted itself out of existence. Perhaps most of the delegates were tired of passing laws that only made things worse. Perhaps they knew their limitations. The man at the podium did not seem to have any limitations. He could probably work miracles.

One impetus for passage of the Enabling Act was the Reichstag Fire of February 1933, a week before the general election that sent veteran and new delegates to the Reichstag. Regardless of who was responsible for the fire, the Communists or the Nazis, it allowed newly appointed Chancellor Hitler to push even more vigorously for passage of the Act. His sole purpose was to increase the number of pro-Act votes in the Reichstag to two-thirds or better, which would ensure passage of the Act. Support came from the Catholic Center Party, whose votes were secured with promises to respect religious freedom. This is somewhat reminiscent of how ObamaCare was passed – with bribes and guarantees of earmarks and not a little support from the American Catholic Church.

Before the fire, the Nazis had polled only twelve percent of the vote. Hitler's decree of a national emergency pushed that up to about forty-four percent. Blaming the Communists, he issued the Reichstag Fire Decree, which suspended most civil liberties in Germany. It enabled him to ban publications considered hostile to the Nazi cause. It also precipitated a reign of terror and intimidation against anyone who voiced doubt about the wisdom of the Enabling Act. This served to increase the Nazis' chances of passage, because many deputies and voters abstained or were prevented from voting by Hitler's paramilitary SA.

Worried that his hold on the government and the country was being jeopardized by the thuggish SA, whose head, Ernst Rohm, insisted that the SA replace the German army, Hitler in June 1934 launched the bloody "Night of the Long Knives" that resulted in the murders of Rohm and hundreds of SA chiefs. Just as Hitler wished to legalize his dictatorship with the Enabling Act, he wished to soften and legitimize the image of the Nazi Party.)

When the Act became law, Hitler dispensed with the Reichstag, a representative body of the electorate. He would not need to answer to it or to the electorate. It became superfluous, an empty ornament and a semi-respectable podium for his subsequent rantings.

Are Americans condemned to repeat that history? It would be heartening if by that it was meant that Americans were going to finish the American Revolution and roll back government spending, abolish the all the parasitical and regulatory alphabet bureaus, agencies and departments in Washington from A Street S.W. to Z Street N.E., get the government out of our lives, pockets, and pants, off our menus, out of our cars, out of hospitals and doctors' offices, out of the schools, and reintroduce the idea of inviolate individual rights and the proper role of government. The Tea Party movement had the potential for firing Congress, just as Americans had fired the British Crown.

What we have *not* witnessed ever since Barack Obama took office in 2009 is anything so arrogant and bold as the kind of "democratic" *coup d'état* staged by Hitler. The move to the Oval Office was loudly orchestrated, just as Hitler's move to the Chancellorship was loudly orchestrated. Instead, Obama has been writing his own Enabling Act piecemeal, in installments, as patiently as completing a jigsaw puzzle.

This puzzle was begun by the likes of Theodore Roosevelt and Woodrow Wilson long, long ago.

One cannot call it anything but an Enabling Act, because it not so much exclusively bestows the president with plenary powers, as shares those powers with Congress with dependable ideological encouragement from the White House, and opaque (i.e., not transparent) horse-trading and log-rolling between it and Congress, coupled with the White House's arm-twisting and brow-beating emissaries. It comes slowly into focus as each new government-caused "crisis" is answered with an expansion of controls and as each piece of the puzzle helps to complete a picture of what Obama knows is its final form.

Obama campaigned, after all, on the platform that he, too, had remedies for a distressed people and nation. He was rather vague and equivocal about what he meant. But people who were enamored of his vision of what the country should be voted for him. His rhetoric resonated with their yearning for the unearned and the miraculous. Visions of sugar plum fairies and stockings stuffed with all sorts of redistributed goodies danced in their heads.

His rhetoric and bogus charisma commanded a near-religious devotion among his supporters that has few historic parallels. The power of John F. Kennedy's appeal and Amiee Semple McPherson's revival tent and radio style comes to mind. Kennedy and McPherson, too, were faith-healers who spoke in tongues. "By its decision to carry out the political and moral cleansing of our public life, the Government is creating and securing the conditions for a really deep and inner religious life."

Really deep? Another sloppy Obamaism? No. It was Hitler urging the Reichstag to pass the Enabling Act. But one can easily imagine those words being spoken by Obama. He probably has. I don't pretend to remember every toxic and rancid drop of dissimulating verbal swill that has been uttered by the man.

I see parallels here between the purge of Rohm and the SA and the announced departures of key Obama appointees. Whether these resignations were voluntary or solicited by Obama is a moot question. Intentional or not, they serve to ameliorate the tangible public hostility to Obama and his administration and create a more conciliatory image of a man unswervingly dedicated to nationwide "community organizing."

But, what is *our* Reichstag Fire? On the face of it, the subprime mortgage meltdown in 2008, and everything that followed. To attempt to recount that debacle would be to lose the reader in a labyrinth of Federal frauds, scams, bailout tarpaulins, and malfeasances that would bewilder Theseus. There would not be enough thread for him to go clear back to Franklin D. Roosevelt's time and then retrace his steps without being assaulted, TSA-style, by Barney Frank's many Minotaurs.

But the subprime collapse served as the excuse to adopt certain "emergency" confiscatory powers, many already in existence but not fully exploited, others created from whole cloth. Capitalism, Wall Street, and Joe the Plumber were blamed, not Federal policies whose illegitimate economic concoctions had been percolating since at least Bill Clinton's administration. Beginning with Jimmy Carter's Community Reinvestment Act, followed by Ronald Reagan and his Alternative Mortgage Transactions Parity Act and the bailouts of the savings and loans under his watch, every president since then has had a hand in stirring the pot in which the frog swims, and both political parties.

Hitler believed in a division of labor. He wanted his devoted cabinet, not the Reichstag, to exercise power and make law. Obama's cabinet appointments emulate the character and pattern, as well. As Germany's economy was warped and woofed by government fiscal, regulatory, and taxation policies together with entitlement programs, so was and has been America's. Obama enlarged his "cabinet" by creating two or so dozen "czars." They would make law, as well, in their particular satrapies, with the sanction of a complicit and ideologically friendly Congress and to the eager applause of a co-opted press.

In Germany, the Enabling Act allowed Hitler to virtually nationalize key industries – in fact, the whole German economy – allowing owners to "own" them but compelling them to take orders and conform to the government's statist priorities. What is the difference then and now? Only the venue and the language. We have a government intent on regulating, if not taking over, numerous realms of private productive activity, from travel to toys to tobacco to diets to the Internet to oil drilling and exploration to food and farming to medical care and insurance.

All of this and more represents only a climax of successive waves of growing government controls, but it took an Obama to orchestrate it – to slam-dunk it, in populist parlance – not in the name of *fascism* (that would be bigoted "profiling"), but of "progressivism." Also known in certain circles whose members remember the past, have learned from it, and who fear its repetition, as incremental socialism. Call it national socialism, if you will. It still means totalitarianism.

One's more immediate enemies are not Obama, or Nancy Pelosi, or Harry Reid, or Barney Frank, or Henry Waxman, but rather those countless American manqués who empower them and in turn are patronized by them, who do not mind being fondled and groped and radiated by the TSA in the name of a national security that is not security at all, but control for the sake of control. These are the people who scoffed at the Tea Party movement and now sneer at defenders of the First, Second, and Fourth Amendments. These are also the same happily ignorant and insouciant people who claim that the "price of liberty" is slavery to the IRS, the FDA, the EPA, the FCC, the FEC, the PPACA, the SEC, *ad infinitum*. Philosophically, morally, they are the original authors of Obama's Enabling Act. They are card-carrying ciphers of the police state, ready to obey and receive their rewards and enjoy their state-granted privileges. They are the altruist and collectivist dhimmis of a secular Islam.

Will the Republicans check the implementation of Obama's Enabling Act? I have my doubts, too, that a beaver dam can contain a freshet. Their willingness to "negotiate," for example, an extension of the Bush tax cuts instills no confidence in me, nor should it in anyone else. As deadly as Obama's emerging Enabling Act might be, is the anti-principle, anti-morality, anti-philosophy of appeasing pragmatism, of cutting a deal to stave off disaster or to retain power. It sanctions and enables the evil that men can do.

As Ayn Rand famously noted in her novel, *Atlas Shrugged*, "In any compromise between food and poison, it is only death that can win. In any compromise between good and evil, it is only evil that can profit."

Will the Republicans be the death of us?

Long live Lady Liberty!

*"Life of Reason," in *Reason in Common Sense*, Scribner's, 1905, page 284.

December 2010

Obama contra *Churchill*

The joke may be on President Barack Obama. One of his first "house cleaning" chores was to order the removal from the White House Oval Office of the bust of Winston Churchill, a temporary gift from Britain in the wake of 9/11, and to replace it in that same spot with one of Abraham Lincoln. After all, didn't Lincoln oversee a calamitous Civil War to free the slaves? One wonders just how well versed Obama is in the speeches of one of his political heroes. Here is an excerpt from a Lincoln speech, cited in Judge Andrew Napolitano's icon-dissolving book on Lincoln, *Dredd Scott's Revenge*, from a debate with Stephen A. Douglas in Illinois in September 1858:

> "I will say then that I am not, nor ever have been, in favor of bringing about in any way the social and political equality of the white and black races – that I am not, nor ever have been, in favor of making voters or jurors of Negroes, nor of qualifying them to hold office, nor to intermarry with white people, and I will say in addition to this that there is a physical difference between the white and black races which I believe forever forbid the two races living together on terms of social and political equality. And in as much as they cannot so live, while they do remain together there must be the position of superior and inferior, and I as much as any other man am in favor of having the superior position assigned to the white race."*

That is just one of many revealing quotations from Lincoln's written record on the issue of slavery. The evidence has been available to scholars for decades. Napolitano's book dissects Lincoln's role in empowering the federal government to override the Constitution and to consciously misinterpret especially the commerce and general welfare clauses in it to excuse its intervention in the economy and to reduce the scope of individual liberty. (See also Napolitano's remarks on the Department of Homeland Security memo of April 7.)

Lincoln's chief motivation for prosecuting the Civil War was to preserve the Union, not to free the slaves. The obvious evil of slavery is not the subject here. We have little to thank Lincoln for. He endorsed the country's first income tax and the first military draft, and suspended habeas corpus. These were precedent-setting exercises of government power to confiscate wealth and life, in pursuit of a "noble cause," emulated later by his successors in office and certainly countenanced by Congress in pursuit of causes arguable less "noble."

Countless other Americans at the time desired to abolish slavery and enlisted in the army and navy for that reason, or were involved in the abolitionist movement, but Lincoln's motivation was highly ambivalent. The myth surrounding Lincoln, one that has been propagated in textbooks for over a century, that he regarded slavery as a moral abomination and fought a war to eradicate it, is no less a myth than the one surrounding Franklin D. Roosevelt, that he saved the country from the alleged excesses of unregulated capitalism. Of course, Obama also admires FDR.

Does Obama value Lincoln for the slavery issue, or for Lincoln's wholesale violations of the Constitution and the ensuing, steady diminution of freedom? If he reveres Lincoln as an emancipator, then he is a posturing fool. If he reveres him as a symbol of a successful usurpation of Constitutional limitations in the guise of "liberation," then he is slyer than most critics have credited him for being.

On the other hand, Obama might have chucked Churchill out because he was a reproach, in that he spoke eloquently against dictators and men who pursued power for the sake of power and had a more contentious political career. Perhaps Obama is better versed in Churchill's speeches than he is in Lincoln's. Or, it may have something to do with Churchill's suppression of the Mau Mau terrorism in colonial Kenya, when Obama's grandfather, Hussein Onyango Obama, was jailed on suspicion of being a Mau Mau subversive. Which, if true, suggests that Obama approves of terrorism and can boast of having a terrorist sympathizer for a relative.

One can even score Churchill for his early praise of Hitler and Mussolini long before World War II. He repudiated and withdrew that praise when he grasped the nature of their tyrannies. Obama's praise is silent. For example, under the pretence of not wanting to "meddle" in the Iranian election turmoil, his remarks have been tepid and reluctant. How can he criticize an authoritarian soul-mate, Mahmoud Ahmadinejad, for having won a rigged election? He and the Democratic Congress have a demonstrable affinity for fascism and are gathering to themselves unprecedented political power over virtually every aspect of American life. Everything – the truth behind the Lincoln and FDR myths and the myth that Obama loves this country and is only trying to save it by emulating his predecessors – is buried beneath the excelsior of irrelevancies and inconsequentials.

(The bust itself, by Sir Jacob Epstein, is an artistic malignity. Churchill's features are barely discernible through a leprous percolation of bumps and swellings, leading one to imagine the work was rescued just in time from a blaze, damaged but still intact. But it is doubtful that Obama's esthetic sense was so offended by the bust that he decided to rid the Oval Office of it.)

In his "The Lights are Going Out" speech of October, 1938, broadcast to the United States, in which he discusses the triumphs of Hitler in Europe, and the victories of fascist Italy and Spain, Churchill had this to say about dictators:

"You see these dictators on their pedestals, surrounded by the bayonets of their soldiers and the truncheons of their police. On all sides they are guarded by masses of armed men, cannons, airplanes, fortifications, and the like – they boast and vaunt themselves before the world, yet in their hearts there is unspoken fear. They are afraid of words and thoughts: words spoken abroad, thoughts stirring at home – all the more powerful because forbidden – terrify them. A little mouse of thought appears in the room, and even the mightiest of potentates are thrown into panic. They make frantic efforts to bar out thoughts and words; they are afraid of the workings of the human mind. Cannons, airplanes, they can manufacture in large quantities; but how are they to quell the natural promptings of human nature, which after all these centuries of trial and progress has inherited a whole armory of potent and indestructible knowledge?"**

In the "A Hush over Europe," August 1939 speech, also broadcast to the U.S., he noted:

"One thing has struck me as very strange, and that is the resurgence of the one-man power after all these centuries of experience and progress. It is curious how the English-speaking peoples have always had this horror of one-man power. They are quite ready to follow a leader for a time, as long as he is serviceable to them; but *the idea of handing themselves over, lock, stock and barrel, body and soul, to one man, and worshipping him as if he were an idol* – that has always been odious to the whole theme and nature of our civilization. The architects of the American Constitution were as careful as those who shaped the British Constitution to guard against the whole life and fortunes, and all the laws and freedom of the nation, being placed in the hands of a tyrant." [*Italics* mine.]

Obama's Cairo speech was his "Munich" gesture. The West, he said, is not at war with Islam. The difference between Neville Chamberlain's capitulation and Obama's, however, is that Chamberlain believed that Hitler's words, promises and signature on a sheet of paper would bring "peace in our time." It is unlikely he saw no radical distinction between Britain and totalitarian Nazi Germany. He simply and disastrously believed that evil was good at its word, that it saw no benefit in war, and that it had exhausted its ambition for conquest and expropriation.

Obama clearly makes no such distinction, nor will he ever make it. Individual rights, liberty, freedom, the rule of law, the sanctity of contract, private property, freedom of speech – these he is dedicated to trampling and extinguishing, so he could see no difference between them and the abject selflessness required of and demanded by Islam. He is envious of anyone who holds absolute power elsewhere in the world – King Abdullah of Saudi Arabia, Hugo Chavez of Venezuela, to name a few – and has a vested interest in Americans "handing themselves over, lock, stock and barrel, body and soul, to one man, and worshipping him as if he were an idol." Has he not managed to achieve that goal among his supporters and the news media?

Those to whom he should show respect, he slights. Those whom he should slight, he gushes over and establishes a grinning rapport with. Those whom he should be wary of – such as the growing portion of the electorate that was never enamored of his alleged charisma and never dazzled by his populist rhetoric, together with those of his supporters who are having second thoughts about him – he is oblivious to, or told by his staff and advisors are merely disaffected with his programs and policies and can be ignored.

The worst one can say about Churchill is that his record is spotty on the issue of totalitarians. He was not in a commanding position when FDR made Stalin and Soviet Russia allies to fight Nazi Germany. Speaking in 1921, Churchill had this to say about Lenin, whom he was never tempted to praise, and the totalitarian slaughter being revealed in the West:

> "He was told that private property existed as the reward of human toil and thrift. He did not believe it. He killed many thousands of people with whom he disagreed, and caused the deaths of many thousands more, in order to find out the truth of that proposition before he came to the conclusion that they were right and he was wrong....Monsieur Lenin then turned his attention to the currency, and, seeing machines making bank notes, he had a flash of pure Communistic genius. He thought that all he had to do to solve the social problem was to keep the machine going as fast as possible. He thought he had thus found a way of making everybody rich, and paying every workman several thousand a year. He destroyed the currency of Russia....He has not yet started on the Ten Commandments – 'Thou shall not steal,' and 'Thou shall do no

murder'….As we watch this terrible panorama of Russian misery, let us abstract a moral which should be a guidance and an aid. Russia cannot save herself by her exertion, but she may at least save other nations by her example. The lesson from Russia, writ in glaring letters, is the utter failure of this Socialist and Communistic theory, and the ruin which it brings to those subjected to its cruel yoke."

The lesson has not been lost on Obama and the Democratic Congress. It is precisely that yoke they are fitting over the necks of Americans. Hopefully, they will be voted out of power in the next general election, or perhaps checkmated in the next round of Congressional contests. But one may be sure of this: that should that happen, he and Congress will do as much damage to this country as they can before vacating the halls and committee rooms of power. Even after the votes have been counted and the winner has been announced, they will try to take what is left of the country with them. The legislation they are hastily writing and enacting now is intended for perpetuity. It will take some kind of revolution to cause its permanent repeal, and the repeal of all such legislation that preceded it.

In her novel *Atlas Shrugged*, Ayn Rand dramatized the workings of the death premise. This point cannot be over-emphasized. If they cannot live to exercise their power, if they cannot reap the benefits of usurpation, if they cannot take satisfaction in the spectacle of men blindly taking orders and in forcing the recalcitrant to act against their will, they will want the country to die. That is, as well and after all, the *jihadist* way. Obama and his allies wish Americans to *submit*, or else perish as a free people. In that respect, they share the goals and means of the Islamists.

Which returns us to 9/11, and Tony Blair presenting President Bush with the Churchill bust, which Obama understandably did not want.

Dredd Scott's Revenge: A Legal History of Race and Freedom in America, by Judge Andrew Napolitano. Nashville: Thomas Nelson, 2009. P. 89.
**All Churchill quotations are from *Never Give In! The Best of Winston Churchill's Speeches*, selected by his grandson, Winston S. Churchill. New York: Hyperion, 2003.

June 2009

Obama Submits

One could devote a career to dissecting President Barack Obama's speech at Cairo University in Egypt on June 4th and point out in detail its numerous errors, fallacies and untruths. One could even dwell on how apparently naïve his is about the nature of Islam, an ignorance of it that is all the more revealing because he claims to have been exposed to Muslim instruction in Indonesia as a child. His patronizing boast of having come from a Kenyan family "that includes generations of Muslims" is utterly irrelevant. A man is not made by his ancestors – not unless he chooses to be.

On minor errors, Daniel Pipes, the prominent authority on Islam, noted that:

> "Barack Obama's mention of 'seven million American Muslims' in the course of his rambling and complex six-thousand-word address to the Muslim world from Cairo symbolizes the whole message….Study after study has found that demographic figure about three times too high. But Islamist organizations like the Council on American-Islamic Relations [CAIR] and the Islamic Society of North America [ISNA] relentlessly promote the notion of seven or even ten million American Muslims. Obama's accepting their version amounts to a giveaway, a cheap way to win the approbation of Islamists who so widely influence Muslim opinion."

In short, Obama was soap-boxing for an American voting bloc. But it would be profitable to first dismiss his assertion that America and Islam are "not exclusive and need not be in competition. Instead they overlap and share common principles, principles of justice and progress, tolerance and the dignity of all human beings," an assertion he echoes throughout the rest of his speech whose theme could only be called, to second Pipes' appraisal, "sucking up to the Muslims."

America and Islam are not only "exclusive," but political and philosophical antipodes. America stands for individual rights, freedom of thought and speech, objective justice, progress, and the liberty to live and conduct one's life without encountering or resorting to force. Islam has never stood for those things, which are in fact objects of its scorn and hostility. Islam is a political/religious ideology that does not tolerate intellectual or religious freedom and which requires of its adherents complete and unquestioning submission to the words and wishes of a ghost and its marauding prophet. Its concept of justice is barbaric and tribal.

Very little of that brutal "justice" as it is practiced in Muslim countries makes headlines in the West; but then again, such murders, mutilations, "honor" killings and the like also occur in the West and the U.S., but do not attract any news coverage, because that would be construed as "stereotyping" Islam and Muslims.

There is no "dignity" to be observed in seeing a single person prostrate himself in obeisance to Mecca, while the spectacle of hundreds performing the same submission is obscene. (It could be humorous; I oft times hope that some comedy group would be brave enough to satirize Islam and Muslims, just as the Monty Python group satirized Christianity.) There is no "dignity" to be observed in Muslim women forced to wear drab, de-sexing traditional garb. Muslims would probably agree with the latter evaluation. What is there in Islam or any of its practitioners to "respect"?

Islam, after the Catholic Church, was the most intolerant creed in history and in existence now. One is either a Muslim, a conquered *kaffir* or *dhimmi* – or dead. Islamists believe in progress only if there is something to loot and that can be had without violating the primitive precepts of the Koran – such as camels, slaves, oil fields, or foreign property – but Islam itself is not by its nature a genesis of progress, nor can it ever be. A moral code that requires the voluntary or enforced stunting or compartmentalization of the mind is not going to invent air-conditioning or nuclear power plants or open heart surgery. It can appropriate the products of a free mind, but never originate them. That makes it a preeminently parasitical ideology.

Islam's chief source of moral authority is the Koran, which, like the Torah and the Bible, is a hodge-podge of fanciful, disparate, and unintegrated casuistic imperatives and fables of questionable moral import. Moreover, it encourages and sanctions holy war or *jihad* against non-believers and their conquest by force or *taqiyya* or deception. There is no theological "subtext" in its exhortations to kill or enslave Jews, Christians and other non-Muslims "wherever you find them"; these and similarly belligerent injunctions throughout the Koran are not euphemistic commands to "love thy neighbor" and "cast not the first stone." They are to be taken literally. The "violent extremists" Obama inveighed against in his speech are only practicing the core tenets of Islam; as I have remarked in past commentaries, remove those tenets from Islam, and what would be left would not be Islam, but a creed as insipid and pacific as that of the Amish.

Yet, the fundamental, anti-mind, anti-philosophy, and anti-moral character of the Koran was selectively overlooked, allowing Obama to quote from it three times during his speech. Those taken-out-of-context nuggets were lifted from a mountain of contaminated verbal slag. But, then, Obama and his aides are not particularly finicky about where they find "wisdom." Look at the composition of his White House staff and the character of his appointees.

In one section of his speech, Obama delivers a series of compliments to "Islam" which are in fact calumnies against the West, in which he credits Islam with technological and medical achievements. But the Arabs who largely rediscovered Greek and Roman thought and science a millennia ago were exceptions to the rule of Islam. "Tolerant" Islam snuffed out the Arab Enlightenment. For an excellent refutation of Obama's assertion that the West owes Islam any kind of cultural debt, see Andy Clarkson's "The United States of America and Islam have nothing fundamental in common."

As ideas, America and Islam *are* mutually exclusive and fundamentally incompatible. There is no reconciliation possible between freedom and servitude, between reason and faith, between progress and stagnation, between the sanctity of property and legalized theft, between individual rights and societies policed by priestly castes. As with reason versus any other faith or religion, it is a matter of "either-or." Obama repeated what he said in Ankara, Turkey in April, that the United States "is not and never will be at war with Islam." That may be true, however, Islam has been and is certainly now at war with the U.S. and with the West. Obama refuses to acknowledge that reality, because, politically, psychologically, and morally, he would be at home in any Muslim society. One can easily imagine him rising through the echelons of such a society to become a power in it or over it.

> "I know that Islam has always been a part of America's story. The first nation to recognize my country was Morocco. In signing the Treaty of Tripoli in 1796, our second president, John Adams, wrote 'The United States has in itself no character of enmity against the laws, religion or tranquility of Muslims.' And since our founding, American Muslims have enriched the United States."

He knows no such thing. One cannot imagine how a collection of undifferentiated manqués can "enrich" any nation. Look at what is happening to Britain and Europe. True, Islam has "always" been a part of America's story in that Muslim pirates preyed on American merchant vessels and Muslim monarchs seized American oil fields. In fact, well into the first quarter of the 19th century, Muslims raided European port towns from Iceland to Ireland to Britain to France and Spain, and in the Mediterranean, for slaves. And, with all due respect to John Adams, he never had to deal personally with Muslims. If he had ever gone to Morocco or Algiers or any other part of the world in which Islam held sway, he might have agreed with Winston Churchill's evaluation a century later of how pathetic and miserable the life of a Muslim was.

Furthermore, given all the research facilities in Washington available to Obama and his speech-writers, one wonders where they find this "history." The treaty of 1786 with Morocco, which implicitly recognized the United States, was secured with what can only be called a bribe of gifts worth $10,000 to the Emperor of Morocco. Had it not been paid, it would have been piracy as usual, in competition with the potentates of Tripoli, Algiers, and Tunis to seize American merchant vessels and hold the crews for ransom.

France was the first nation to recognize the United States as an independent nation, when it assisted the Revolution with money, troops, and naval support. Britain necessarily recognized the U.S. when it agreed in 1782 to negotiate a treaty with the "13 U.S.," signed in Paris in 1783 and ratified by Congress in 1784. Next to recognize the U.S. was the Netherlands. For a summary account of American relations with the Barbary States, see the Avalon Project at Yale Law School.

See also my commentaries, **Barbary Pirates: Old and New**, on Rule of Reason, from August 2007; **The Janus Face of Islam** from September 2006; or **Our Islamic Nemesis, Then and Now** from August 2006 for further discussions of the impossibility of "peace" with Islam, a political/religious ideology fundamentally and necessarily driven to conquest by the same psychopathic forces that drove Nazism, with which Islamic leaders sympathized then and probably still do, although they are keeping that under their headdresses. The paramilitary organizations of Hamas and Hezbollah have adopted the Nazi military parade style; their mass salutes are merely closed-fist versions of the Nazi "Sieg heil."

The latter subject is not one much known in this country. Muslim hatred of the Jews in the Middle East predates World War I. Amin el-Husseini, the Grand Mufti of Jerusalem, was especially eager to exterminate Jews in Palestine and personally discussed the project with Hitler. Saudi Arabia was another pro-Nazi sympathizer. In point of fact, I cannot recall a single Middle Eastern, 20th century dictator or strongman who at one time or another had not expressed admiration for the Nazis, except, perhaps, the Shah of Iran (the son, 1919-1980). For a revealing account of how the Nazis planned to exploit the Arab "liberation movement" by assigning special military units to the region to direct the Middle Eastern branch of the Holocaust, see Klaus-Michael Mallmann and Martin Cuppers' "'Elimination of the Jewish National Home in Palestine': The Einsatzkommando of the Panzer Army Africa, 1942." These units were modeled on the ones that directed the massacres of Jews in Poland,

Czechoslovakia and Russia, or aided in rounding them up for transport to the death camps.

Before flying to Cairo, Obama stopped in Saudi Arabia to "consult" with King Abdullah, the creature he bowed to at the London summit. Saudi Arabia and its repressive Wahhabist monarchy are ample proof that Islam can only appropriate the products of free minds, not originate or create them, in this instance, having seized Western created oil fields and investing the loot from them in the West. And, one must question Obama's apparent fascination with the Saudis. Is it rooted in power-envy, or an obsession founded on pragmatism?

"Saudi Arabia and the United States have a near 60-year-old relationship based on guaranteeing oil supplies in return for U.S. protection for the Saudi monarchy."

The "relationship" can only be characterized as extortionate, one made possible by American willingness to prop up a medieval oligarchy by prohibiting the development of oil deposits in the U.S. One can bet that the Saudis have an army of well-paid lobbyists in Washington who ensure that an "environmentally conscious" Congress perpetuates that extortion.

It is a significant clue to how receptive the 3,000 guests at Cairo University who listened to Obama were to the idea of coexisting with Jews and Israel when they remained silent and unresponsive when he touched on anti-Semitism, the Holocaust and Buchenwald. As one ABC correspondent remarked, "You could've heard a pin drop." But each statement of capitulation and compromise earned him applause. Every Islamist knows that a "two-state" solution to the Israeli-Palestinian conflict is but a formula for bringing about the destruction of Israel. Obama, Secretary of State Hillary Clinton and their policymakers do not know it. Or perhaps they do, but are counting on "empathy" to prevent it from happening.

All this is aside from the manner in which Obama began his address to the Muslim world.

> "We meet at a time of great tension between the United States and Muslims around the world, tension rooted in historical forces that go beyond any current policy debate. The relationship between Islam and the West includes centuries of coexistence and cooperation but also conflict and religious wars."

You can't get more Marxist-Hegelian than that. America and Islam are thesis and antithesis struggling against each other in what must ultimately result in a tension-releasing starburst of collectivist union – of pure communism, or socialism, or fascism, or a global caliphate, or whatever facilitates "global amity" and animates our "collective conscience." This belief in the mystical powers of "coexistence and cooperation" and wishing they would work, of course, is stressed by Obama in his assertion that "Islam has demonstrated through words and deeds the possibilities of religious tolerance and racial equality." That assertion must have provoked disgust in the defenders of the West, and laughter among Islamists.

What is Obama's solution? What rain dance of his is expected to promote the climax of those impersonal "historical forces"? Not ideas. Not principles. Not the assertion of reason and rights. But "dialogue." That is, compromise and give-and-take. It cannot mean anything else but have-not Muslims negotiating what they will take from the haves, and Islamists looting the carcass of Israel. It also means, as Obama stated, pouring more billions of dollars into the corrupt cesspool economies of Pakistan and Afghanistan and other areas of Islamist hegemony. "Humanity" and Immanuel Kant will it; Obama is dutifully unmindful of the deleterious consequences to the West. Or, perhaps not.

There is so much more in Obama's Cairo speech that could be dissected. All his verbiage about freedom of religion, freedom of speech, "human rights" and "democracy" is just one pre-packaged, mandatory shibboleth undercut by his demonstrable penchant for statism. In summary, however, his speech was one which George W. Bush himself could have delivered. It simply reaffirmed the evasive, non-judgmental, accommodating policies of the Bush years and broadened their scope.

It was a defining act of submission.

June 2009

In Congress, Ignorance is Strength

I open this commentary with the introduction to my previous commentary, "The Mainstream Smearing of Ayn Rand." The disparity in subject is not so irrelevant as one might presume, but I won't dwell on that matter.

Speaker of the House Nancy Pelosi looked like a deer caught in the blinding headlight of an oncoming freight train, her expression frozen in either ignorance or fear. It has always been difficult to distinguish between the two in her. But the malice in her words was palpable.

CNSNews.com: "Madam Speaker, where specifically does the Constitution grant Congress the authority to enact an individual health insurance mandate?"

Pelosi: "Are you serious? Are you serious?"

CNSNews.com: "Yes, yes, I am."

Pelosi then shook her head before taking a question from another reporter. Her press spokesman, Nadeam Elshami, then told CNSNews.com that asking the speaker of the House where the Constitution authorized Congress to mandate that individual Americans buy health insurance was not a "serious question."

"You can put this on the record," said Elshami. "That is not a serious question. That is not a serious question."

His iterating mockery of the reporter is indeed on the record. Elshami, deputy communications director and senior adviser to Pelosi, later issued a press release stating that Congress was empowered by the commerce clause in the Constitution to mandate individual health insurance. The chairman of the Senate Judiciary Committee, Patrick Leahy (D-Vermont), however, differed from that dubious specificity, instead likening the power to compel all Americans to buy health insurance to federal authority to impose speed limits on interstate highways (???), adding that "nobody questions" Congress's authority to impose controls of any kind. House Majority Leader Steny Hoyer (D-Maryland) linked the power to the general welfare clause.

Since that demonstration of Congressional arrogance, the House passed its health-care legislation by a vote of 220 to 215, squeaking through only because of the browbeating of Blue Dog Democrats by the

Pelosi gang. Hardly a glittering victory. The bill has been sent to the Senate, which has its own versions of health care legislation to scuffle over. The House bill, remarked Senator Lindsey Graham of South Carolina remarked, soon after Speaker of the House Nancy Pelosi and her determined co-conspirators posed with smiles of triumph for photo ops, was "dead on arrival." In the meantime, Senator Joe Lieberman of Connecticut issued his own warning:

> If a government plan is part of the deal, "as a matter of conscience, I will not allow this bill to come to a final vote," said Sen. Joe Lieberman, the Connecticut independent whose vote Democrats need to overcome GOP filibusters.

It seems that some Senators understand the original purpose of the Senate, which is to act as a check on the populist, "democratic," majority-rule grounded legislation concocted by the House, to better preserve and protect the life, liberty, property and pursuit of happiness of Americans. Unfortunately, only Graham, Lieberman, and a handful of other Senators appreciate that intention. Others have publicly articulated it – but with reservations.

> Sen. Daniel Akaka (D-Hawaii) says he is "not aware" of the Constitution giving Congress the authority to make individuals purchase health insurance, as the health care bills in both the House and Senate require.

No, he isn't aware of the Constitution mandating Congress the power to force Americans to buy health insurance. And that unawareness won't stop him from advocating such compulsion.

When asked if there was a specific part of the Constitution that gives Congress the authority to make people buy health insurance, Akaka said: "Not in particular with health insurance. It's not covered in that respect. But in ways to help citizens in our country to live a good life, let me say it that way, is what we're trying to do, and in this case, we're trying to help them with their health."

> Both House and Senate health care bills mandate that people buy health insurance, facing a financial penalty if they do not. Akaka said this mandate should not be looked upon as a penalty…"It's an idea of making it possible for people and this is what it's all about," he said. "I don't look upon that as a penalty but as a way of getting help with health insurance."

If Akaka had been sharp enough, he might have echoed House Majority Leader Steny Hoyer of Maryland and claimed that "helping people" at the point of a gun to buy health insurance came under the (misunderstood) general welfare clause. But, he was not sharp enough, and that neglect simply added to his ignorance quotient.

Other politicians have been more specific in their opposition to any health care legislation. Senator Orrin Hatch of Utah remarked that if the government can force Americans to purchase health insurance, "then there is literally nothing the federal government can't force us to do."

Senator Jack Reed of Rhode Island is in a dead heat with Senator Akaka in being unaware of any Constitutional mandate to compel Americans to buy health insurance. When asked by a reporter to identify that mandate in the Constitution, Reed answered:

> "Let me see," said Reed. "I would have to check the specific sections, so I'll have to get back to you on the specific section. But it is not unusual that the Congress has required individuals to do things, like sign up for the draft and do many other things too, which I don't think are explicitly contained [in the Constitution]. It gives Congress a right to raise an army, but it doesn't say you can take people and draft them. But since that was something necessary for the functioning of the government over the past several years, the practice on the books, it's been recognized, the authority to do that."

The gentleman did not "get back" to the reporter who buttonholed him with that question. He likened the element of compulsion to forcing Americans to register for the military draft. That is okay with him. It is all about duty, and sacrifice, and "giving back" to society. Senator Ben Nelson of Nebraska also displayed his ignorance as well as his manners:

> "Specifically, where in the Constitution does Congress get its authority to mandate that individuals purchase health insurance?" CNSNews.com asked Nelson.

> "Well, you know, I don't know that I'm a constitutional scholar," said Nelson. So, I, I'm not going to be able to answer that question." The senator then turned away to answer another reporter's question.

If he doesn't know whether or not he's a constitutional scholar, then he isn't one. That answer invites the observation and question: One can expect members of the House of Representatives to be foggy on matters of constitutionality, although their two-year terms ought to allow them to become experts on the subject.

Should Senators come to their jobs as Solons prepared to repel any and all usurpations of the Constitution? Yes. Willing and able to uphold individual rights and the sanctity of private contract? Yes. It is in the nature of the title and the concomitant responsibility of the office. Most senators, however, do not come to the job with anything near a tenuous knowledge of their function. And many of them assume their seats in the Senate with a contempt for the Constitution that may as well be ignorance.

Most Senators complement their ignorance of the Constitution with an indifference to its clearly-worded stipulations, and in this state of mind emulate President Barack Obama, former pseudo-professor of Constitutional law at the University of Chicago Law School. Obama is not so much ignorant of that document as hostile to it. It is "deeply flawed," and a "charter of negative liberties," which should be amended or rewritten to include the "positive" liberties of welfare state entitlements and provisions for fiat executive powers. His demonstrated hostility for individual rights and private property is arguably more deep-seated than was FDR's, whose grasp of the Constitutional limits placed on the executive and legislative branches of government was as blithely disjointed as is Obama's.

The key to understanding the machinations of Obama, Pelosi, Reid and their allies in Congress is to grasp this: No one can express, as they have, such vehement ignorance without knowing full well what it is they are ignorant of.

It is time Americans called their bluff, as they may well do in the 2010 mid-term elections, or in manners reminiscent of the Tea Parties of 2009, or of the Minute Men of 1775.

November 2009

Parsing Obama

To grasp the magnitude of the national debt Obama (and his Republican predecessor) has been ringing up, a comparison should help illustrate the task. Bernard Madoff's robbery and defrauding investors of some $50 billion can be represented by the diameter of the solar system. The federal government, using the *same scamming* tactics, is amassing a debt about the diameter of the Milky Way galaxy. Madoff's scheme can be measured in millions of miles. The federal government's, in almost limitless parsecs. That measurement ought to suffice to dramatize the scale of the hole he is deliberately digging for the country in his role as Community-Organizer-in-Chief.

Since it is only productive work – whether in a factory making widgets, or in a research lab creating new medicines or computer software – that gives the dollar bill its value, Obama's galactic debt will be expected to be funded from taxes paid from the productive, private sector. I make that distinction because the government is non-productive; it produces nothing, not even the paper its one hundred thousand commandments are printed on, not even the pens with which presidents sign legislation into law. That growing, astronomical debt, however, will serve to shrink the productive sector and make it less productive in exponential leaps and bounds – off a cliff. It must inexorably reach a point that the productive sector can no longer sustain the debt it is expected to pay. Then we will have reached the economic status of, say, Zimbabwe.

The sentencing of Madoff to 150 years in prison for his crime elicited an outpouring of sanctimonious news coverage, complete with quotations from angry victims of his scheme and a sated passion for justice. Of course, Madoff deserved his sentence. Given his age, 71, perhaps he will serve just ten of it before dying in prison.

What clashes with the news media coverage of Madoff's trial, conviction and sentencing for his crime is the studied obtuseness of the news media for the same crime being committed by the government. Madoff, you see, was "greedy" or "avaricious," and that, according to the morality of altruism and selflessness, is immoral and antisocial. The government, however, is committing the same crime, but that is in order to "do good." So its orgy of debt-creation, its extortionate policies of roping all Americans into a "dog-eat-dog" welfare state, and its targeting the most productive and the wealthiest in society for special punishment, are all acceptable and laudable.

Even though the news media has knowledge of this multi-trillion dollar scam, that knowledge elicits not an iota of outrage among the photogenic news anchors and highly paid print pundits. No respectable TV

106

or print journalist even thinks of the scam in terms of a continuing and expanding bilking of Americans from their wealth, investments and taxes. (Except, perhaps, John Stossel of ABC, whose "20/20" report on the cost and dishonesty of the proposed socialist health care program was conveniently cancelled and replaced with a special on the life and death of Michael Jackson – as though we weren't already gagging on the nonstop adulatory and scandal sheet coverage of this very disturbed person.)

"There is no plea agreement," Assistant U.S. Attorney Marc Litt said at the hearing, meaning Madoff must plead guilty to 11 counts that he now faces in a criminal information filed today. Madoff is charged with securities fraud, investment advisor fraud, mail fraud, wire fraud, three counts of money laundering, false statements, perjury, false filings with the U.S. Securities and Exchange Commission and theft from an employee benefit plan, Litt said.

No one is calling for the indictments of Barney Frank, Nancy Pelosi, Christopher Dodd, Henry Waxman, and all the usual suspects in Congress and the White House, even though they are all parties to the same crime. Examine the definitions of each of the counts with which Madoff was charged and convicted of, and ask how the actions of the co-conspirators differ any from what Madoff was found guilty of. One fundamental difference between Madoff's crime and the federal government's is that Madoff did not employ direct, legalized force to take his victims' money. Another is that it was not in Madoff's agenda to make his victims dependent on his benefice. In court, when he faced his victims, he (rather belatedly) apologized to them, and did not say, "But I did it for your sakes."

"The U.S. government gets funds in three ways. It can look for increased revenues (through higher taxes). It can look to cut expenses (through lower spending). Or it can borrow by issuing new Treasury bonds. Replacing old bonds with new bonds is called "rolling over the debt," and is done every day by households, businesses, and governments."

Which of these ways will the Obama administration adopt to raise revenue? Count out number two. The productive sector of the economy will be expected to fund numbers one and three – for as long as it survives.

On July 4th, President Barack Obama sent a holiday greeting to his supporters, via the Democratic National Committee. Obama's presumptuousness, of course, knows no bounds or limits. His July 4th greeting was all about the importance of Independence Day. This commentary will examine the fallacies and fabrications contained in his greeting. At first glance, the message appears vacuous and commonplace. But beneath its blandness is poison.

*This weekend, our family will join millions in celebrating
America. We will enjoy the glow of fireworks, the taste of
barbeque, and the company of good friends. As we all celebrate
this weekend, let's also remember the remarkable story that led to
this day.*

The story that led to the 4th of July is not merely "remarkable," it
is epochal. It is the story of men who decided that the idea that they owned
their own lives, and not a tyrant, must be taken seriously enough to sever
all political ties with that tyrant. What is Obama doing today? Taking
actions to guarantee that our lives are tied to his whims and wishes, just as
they were with Old World tyrants. If he had any valid recollection of that
"remarkable story," he would see that he is the villain.

*Two hundred and thirty-three years ago, our nation was born when
a courageous group of patriots pledged their lives, fortunes and
sacred honor to the proposition that all of us are created equal.*

No. They pledged themselves to the proposition that men (not
politically correct "all of us") should exist in a state of freedom and not in
one of subservience. Here is an instance of how disconnected Obama and
his allies in Congress are from not only history, but from reality – and how
indifferent or hostile they are to that history and to reality. It is precisely
the lives, fortunes and sacred honor of Americans that they are so busy
expropriating, redistributing or destroying. The certain rights of life,
liberty, the pursuit of happiness and property are to them not unalienable,
but disposable and eminently open to violation in the name of the "public
good." It is their operating premise that whenever any form of government
becomes destructive of the ends of government, that is, to securing
individual rights and deriving its limited powers from the consent of the
governed, the people have no right to alter or abolish that government, or
even to criticize it.

*Our country began as a unique experiment in liberty – a bold,
evolving quest to achieve a more perfect union. And in every
generation, another courageous group of patriots has taken us one
step closer to fully realizing the dream our founders enshrined on
that great day.*

No, the United States did not begin as a "unique experiment in
liberty." It began as an assertion of that liberty. No, a "more perfect union"
was not the end of the Founders, but the establishment of a government
that could best guarantee life, liberty, property, and the pursuit of

happiness. A "more perfect union" to Obama is all Americans marching in lockstep to an ideal collectivist state. "Quests" do not "evolve," not unless one is not certain of one's end. And ever since the Civil War, generations of politicians and political thinkers have been moving away from the end that our Founders sought to achieve. It takes no courage to advocate slavery and servitude to a confused and ignorant citizenry.

> *Today, all Americans have a hard-fought birthright to a freedom which enables each of us, no matter our views or background, to help set our nation's course. America's greatness has always depended on her citizens embracing that freedom – and fulfilling the duty that comes with it.*

It is that "hard-fought birthright" which Obama the constitutional "scholar" is busily cheating us out of with the skill of a shyster lawyer. Ideas set a nation's course and determine its future or its fate. Freedom and duty are literal antipodes. No one has a duty to sanction his own servitude or slavery, which is what Obama is advocating as the "price" of the freedom he is hurriedly destroying and which he hopes we do not embrace so selfishly that we will not relinquish it to satisfy the democratic mob and to perpetuate the comfort and peace of mind of a corrupt, prostituted Congress.

> *As a free people, we must each take the challenges and opportunities that face this nation as our own. As long as some Americans still must struggle, none of us can be fully content. And as America comes ever closer to achieving the perfect union our founders dreamed, that triumph – that pride – belongs to all of us.*

Obama's challenges and opportunities to expand federal power are not those of Americans who value their freedom. Americans must always "struggle" to achieve their personal happiness, and can be content with having achieved it without being asked to live for the sake of others. That happiness cannot be achieved if men are chained to each other's needs.

> *So today is a day to reflect on our independence, and the sacrifice of our troops standing in harm's way to preserve and protect it. It is a day to celebrate all that America is. And today is a time to aspire to all we can still become.*

> *With very best wishes, President Barack Obama July 4th, 2009*

Yes, many Americans are reflecting upon their independence, not only on that of this country, but on their independence from each other as individuals who own their own lives and pursue their own happiness – which is not what Obama is asking of either our troops or any Americans. Sacrifice for unselfish, altruist ends is what he promotes – not the defense of this country, not its prosperity, not its freedom. That reflection by many thoughtful, concerned Americans has been deemed "right wing extremism" by the Department of Homeland Security deserving of surveillance, scrutiny, and police action.

In summary, one must agree in spirit with conservative columnist Charles Krauthammer that it is not Obama's words that one must pay attention to, but what he does. But one must disagree with Krauthammer because collectivism is what he and the Democrats have been quite obviously preaching for the last two years. One merely needs to read between the lines and the lies.

July 2009

Freedom of Speech

Free Speech vs. Blasphemy:
Thoughts on the Danish Cartoons of Mohammed

"As we trace the genius of a nation by their taste in poetry and music, so by their encouragement of these we may judge of their rise or fall; good authors have never been wanting in happy climes. Barbarism begins her reign by banishing the Muses. Those who have ears to hear, let them hear!"

So wrote Philip Dormer Stanhope, the Earl of Chesterfield, in 1749 in a preface to a pamphlet of his speech in the House of Lords against the proposed Act for Licensing the Stage, an act supported by politicians who were being mocked in theaters by satire to the applause of an appreciative public.

In a not so coincidental dovetailing of events, a bill to regulate "hate speech" is at present being debated in the British parliament that would make it a criminal offense to publicly disparage any creed or set of religious beliefs, in addition to "inciting" violence via words or pictures against members of any race or religious sect. Ostensibly, the bill is aimed at Muslims who call for *jihad* in Britain; in effect, it will silence anyone who questions or criticizes any creed or system of beliefs. The bill aims to suppress the provocation of thugs and rioters by gagging those who would call them thugs and rioters.

It will silence everyone but the Muslims.

At the same time, the Muslim "furor" over the publication and republication in Danish and European newspapers of cartoons that caricature Mohammed, whose depiction in any form is regarded as blasphemy, shocked many Westerners from their multicultural apathy. The one cartoon that seems to have touched the Muslim nerve – shall we call it "sensitivity"? – shows the head of Mohammed wearing a turban shaped as a lit-fuse bomb. This was a caricature that summed up the thousands of murders and scale of destruction wrought by Islamic "martyrs" and jihadists over the past thirty years. It was an astute, stylistic observation, a justifiable estimate of the means and ends of Islamic fascism.

The pit felt at the bottom of many stomachs over this new demand of the Muslims is *fear*: fear of mindless retribution, of death and destruction. It causes those who feel it to shut up in the name of "respect" for Muslim beliefs. This is the true nature of the "respect" of major American news organizations, such as CBS, when it refused to show a single cartoon.

The pit felt at the bottom of other stomachs is resolve, of a determination to stand up now for the freedom to say what one thinks, with the knowledge that if the West capitulates to Muslim demands, it will have surrendered the key freedom that permits the fight for all the other freedoms. Many European newspapers have defied Muslim "sensibilities" and reprinted the cartoons.

Islamic spokesmen called this action a "provocation." But what is it that is being "provoked"? Violence. Property destruction. Kidnappings. Murders. The initiation of physical force and terror. All in the name of Mohammed and Allah. Hardly the behavior of a "pacific" religion that would persuade one that it just wants to "get along."

Implied in the claim that images of Mohammed constitute blasphemy, is that *anyone* who creates such an image is guilty of blasphemy. **What the Muslims are demanding is that *non-Muslims* accept that religious tenet.** Thus, "respect" by non-Muslims of the tenet, at the price of surrendering the right to criticize Islam, means *virtual* conversion to Islam, a major step in the direction of *actual* conversion.

Islamists see the implications of multiculturalism and "diversity" much better than do the advocates and practitioners of these secular "creeds." Islamists are infamous for not subscribing to multiculturalism and diversity. They might claim that it is not conversion they seek, but "respect." But if one does not "respect" a belief, it is one's right to question it, or to criticize it in a book, essay, speech, or cartoon. However, if one "respects" it, then it becomes a taboo subject, off limits to reasoned enquiry and civil discussion. One tells oneself: I have no right to say anything about it. And if one is prohibited, under penalty of prosecution, intimidation, or physical violence, from saying or writing anything about it, then there is no reason or point to thinking of it, either.

What a formula for thought control!

The Islamists know it. Most Western politicians and intellectuals do not.

It is time that Muslims here and abroad got used to "offensive" portrayals of Mohammed, and, for good measure, of Allah himself. After all, no one is forcing them to look at the cartoons. The West regularly shrugs off the pictorial vilification of Western institutions, culture, creeds, persons and icons. Anyone familiar with the Arab press and Arab websites will note how vicious Muslim cartoonists are.

That would be a fair trade, would it not, an exercise in mutual "tolerance" and good will? One might say that the solution to the problem is reciprocity. The Arab press can publish vicious cartoons of the West, and the West can publish mildly "offensive" cartoons about Islam.

But it is not an issue of reciprocity. Reciprocity is not in the Islamic agenda. "Islam" means "submission," and it is submission its ill-willed mullahs and imams demand in exchange for the "peace" of intellectual torpidity in their rank and file followers, as well as in the West. Islam is by its very nature intolerant of other creeds and requires absolute, mindless obedience of Allah and compliance with the prophet's commandments. It cannot be "reformed" as Christianity has been. Even the new Pope, Benedict XVI, has conceded that. There are no concessions Islam could possibly make without triggering its self-destruction. Fundamentally, there is no such thing as a "moderate" Muslim or a "civilized" Islam, not when the core beliefs of the Koran and commands of the Hadith sanction the murder and enslavement of non-Muslims in an on-going jihad that will end only with the establishment of a global caliphate.

Islamic spokesman claim that they do not seek to crush freedom of speech or expression, only to put "limits" on it. Ultimately, however, any "limit" on speech means no expression, no freedom to say what one thinks must be said. It means not reaching a conclusion, and settling for only half a syllogism, or none at all. It means that an idea has been removed from debate, discussion, and criticism.

This is a defining moment for the West. It must either speak up in defense and in bold, unapologetic assertion of the idea of freedom of speech, or forever cringe in "respect" of Islamic tenets, much as in the film *The Godfather*, the favor-seeking mortician cringed when gangster Vito Corleone accused him of not granting him "respect." The fearful mortician immediately offered his respect and submission. He was seeking mere vengeance; Corleone required submission and acknowledgement of his power.

This will logically require the ultimate scrapping of another "belief" system, that of multiculturalism and diversity, and their recognition as fatal fallacies.

The genius of the West has been ever since the Renaissance a commitment to the freedom of men to question the moral claims of others. Reason has always settled the question. Islamists are demanding that the

West banish the Muse of Reason. Let those who have ears, hear that demand and understand its fundamental requirement. And let those who understand it, speak now, or forever maintain a "respectful" silence.

February 2006

Towards Freedomless Speech

It is not so curious that in the wake of the Danish cartoon conflict, during which the American press and news media revealed their tepid commitment to freedom of speech and the inviolacy of the First Amendment, incidents of assaults on that freedom would not only multiply, but assume odd but no less ominous forms.

In 1996, in "The Ghouls of Grammatical Egalitarianism," a review for The Social Critic of the Association of American University Press's *Guidelines for Bias-Free Writing*, I noted:

> "Thought orthodoxy is not synonymous with thought control. There is no Federal Board of Language Usage to which publishers must submit their books and journals to be tested for discriminatory or disparaging language before they can be put on the market for sale to the public. However, while no official agency of control exists, there is a kind of interlocking directorate of semi-public institutions and organizations which accomplishes the same purpose by presenting a united front against freedom of expression and imposing orthodoxy on our culture's intellectual and literary pacesetters. 'Say what you please, we're not censors!....But say it *our* way, or do not bother to say it.'

> "Short of overt government repression, I cannot imagine a more insidious form of thought control than this, which is to thrust independent minds of whatever professional suasion or degree of ability into a purgatory that is not quite freedom and not quite slavery."

And, in discussing the ramifications of the Telecommunications Act of 1996 in my entry on "Censorship" in the 2002 edition of *The Encyclopedia of Library and Information Science* (Vol. 70), I observed:

> "All the provisions regarding 'obscenity' are ostensibly for the sake of protecting children. An early precedent for this particular ruse was the Rubbish and Smut bill (or the Schund und Schmutz law) of May 1927, enacted by the Weimar government in Germany, in which children under the age of 18 were similarly 'protected' by controls from plays, literature, art, and especially nightclub performances that might corrupt their moral fiber. The act took the form of a ban of all under 18 years of age from

proximity to these 'evils.' It also gave the police the unlimited power to enter private residences to enforce the law, and even prohibited young adults from attending art classes that employed nude models. The Rubbish and Smut law was an overture to wholesale Nazi censorship six years later."

Germany was prepared for Nazi rule in more ways than one – chiefly by its philosophy – and the Rubbish and Smut law was passed and enforced in the name of "decency." In the U.S., such laws are enacted on federal and state levels for the same reason, and also in the name of "fairness," "balance," and "sensitivity." Not to mention that Trojan horse of all regulations, bans, and controls: children.

"Speech codes" have established stultifying purgatories of expression not only on college campuses, but in other venues, as well, such as business and even tourism. In how many numberless places of business would one now risk a sexual harassment lawsuit by paying a colleague a compliment on his or her appearance, and probable dismissal by one's employer, who would likely be named a co-defendant for not having enforced federal and state "guidelines"?

And what better way to ensure that college students become "responsible" citizens than by creating lists of "protected" and "unprotected" speech, and even linking academic success to the degree to which students adhere to them? Establish in their minds the habit of observing arbitrary parameters of speech and thought, and they won't give the authorities much trouble. They will be too busy "giving back to society" to discover how much liberty that society has surrendered and taken from them.

And, just the other day, browsing through some Colonial Williamsburg teachers' brochures that offer literature on how to introduce students to the American Revolution, I encountered the term "tradespeople" in lieu of "tradesmen." What the first term conveys is that the men who made the Revolution possible were androgynous "persons" who wore strange clothing and practiced odd customs. But the employment of sanitized terminology is not the worst offense committed by Colonial Williamsburg. Its acceptance of federal grants disqualifies the foundation from teaching anything about why the Revolution occurred, for with the grants come the requirements of political correctness, which can only influence how it represents history.

To return to thought control. The "control" that enforces "orthodoxy" in speech by individuals is simply fear of retribution, reprisal, or financial and personal ruin. To work, thought or speech control relies exclusively on self-censorship. The instances of operable thought control are as ubiquitous and innocuous in our culture as countless drops of water falling on one's forehead in a Chinese torture.

Now, there's a "disparaging" analogy! Could it be construed as an ethnic slur, or a cultural slur? A sleazy lawyer could make a case for both and take me to the cleaners. Wait! Now I'm offending lawyers! *And* cleaners! Well, how about saying that thought control is much like the embrace of an iron maiden? No, that wouldn't sit well with maidens reading this, either. Not that any girl or woman today wouldn't feel offended by being called a "maiden." How about risking being hauled before a Spanish Inquisition for speech heresy? Or for playing Russian Roulette with one's mouth? Nope. I might offend Hispanics, Catholics, or the Moscow Mafia. And perhaps Italians.

A friend remarked to me, referring to the disgraceful behavior of our government and press during the Danish cartoon "outrage," that "Mohammed was only the beginning." Rather, Mohammed is only the capstone of an edifice otherwise known as an Orwellian Ministry of Truth, under construction in our culture for the last half century.

I trust I have made my point. The Mohammedan enforcer of politically correct speech is ready with his scimitar, watching your every movement and listening to your every word, eager to behead unrepentant infidels of the First Amendment. "Slay them wherever you find them." Or take them to court.

And if we are tempted to speak out of turn – that is, to endorse or criticize a candidate for political office and consequently violate the time strictures of the Campaign Finance Law and an arbitrary ruling of the Federal Election Commission – we must not think that law is an abridgement of the First Amendment, but rather as a gag for the "public good."

In Boulder, Colorado, for example, citizens concerned about the "decency" of their neighbors, coworkers, or strangers may have the chance to snitch anonymously to the authorities if they believe a "hate crime" has been committed.

> The Denver Post reports that "the Boulder City Council will take up the matter of allocating public funding for a 'hate hotline,' which would give residents an opportunity to report incidents in which Boulderites use tactless language."

As though that were not bad enough, try to unravel the illogic of a spokesman for the American Civil Liberties Union. The Post reports him as saying, "Our concern – and there are many – is that there is no confidentiality, no legal confidentiality," explains Judd Golden, chairman of the Boulder ACLU. "So it's potentially chilling if people think they are providing this information in confidence and then that information were provided to the government or the government sought access to it. That would chill free speech."

Here is that gibberish unraveled. Golden is not concerned about the power of the government to punish someone for speaking his mind and asserting his freedom of speech. That it has such power, or is seeking it, is the given he sanctions. He is concerned about the jeopardy in which *informants* might find themselves if the government knew *their* identities. It is not the principle of the First Amendment that he is worried can be chilled, splintered, and melted away, but the contextless "freedom of speech" and "privacy" of *petit* Nazis and would-be gauleiters.

The Boulder Council, flailing about in its own shrunken epistemology, believes it has a duty to protect tattletales from any consequences of their "public spirited" actions. Its resolution would not only condemn "the usual individual or collective acts of racism and bigotry," writes the Post, but those who attack, disparage, or denigrate "personal beliefs and values."

Sound familiar? This is Mohammed in the guise of any random soccer mom, public school teacher, community activist, or other endorser of the idea of "hate crimes."

The criminal code and justice system were once legitimately concerned with determining and punishing criminal *actions* in order to protect or uphold individual rights. The concept of "hate crimes," however, extends and sanctions the power of government and our courts to punish *thought,* as well, that is, for *why* a crime *might* have been committed.

It is but a short step from linking an actual crime with "hate" to making it a crime to "hate." One need not *act* on that "hate" to be pilloried by a law or society, except to express one's opinion or position, no matter how rational or irrational it might be. The Boulder Council seems to want to take that step. One can only imagine in how many other American cities that willingness exists in the minds of "stewards of the public good and safety."

On a fundamental cultural level, it is no coincidence that the introduction and gradual acceptance of the concept of "hate crimes" paralleled the stealthy and de facto imposition of politically correct speech. Politically correct speech, in turn, has established the grounds for punishable "tactless language."

In May of 1765, Patrick Henry urged the Virginia General Assembly to adopt the "tactless language" of his Resolves over the "politically correct" style of his time to protest the Stamp Act. When other colonial Americans read that language, deemed by the fearful as "disrespectful," "insensitive," "disparaging" and "offensive" to the majesty and prerogatives of the British Crown, it moved them to unite for the first time to oppose and resist Parliamentary power. *That* was the true beginning of the American Revolution.

The growing silence you hear now is a cowed nation exercising its freedomless speech.

Other articles by the author on censorship:

"Here Comes a Chopper to Chop Off Your Head: Freedom of Expression vs. Censorship in America" Essay: The Journal of Information Ethics (St. Cloud State University, MN/ McFarland & Co., Publishers, Jefferson, NC), Fall 1995

"Patrick Henry: Not Merely an Orator" Essay: *The Colonial Williamsburg Journal*, Winter 1995

"The Ghouls of Grammatical Egalitarianism" a review of *Guidelines for Bias-Free Writing*, ed. Marilyn Schwartz and the Task Force on Bias-Free Language, The Social Critic, November/ December 1996

"Censorship" Entry: *The Encyclopedia of Library and Information Science*, ed. Allen Kent, Marcel Dekker, New York, Vols. 62 (1998) and 70 (2002)

May 2006

"High Noon" for the First Amendment

Most of President Barack Obama's administration cohorts have a distinctly and undeniable leftist hue, ranging from Marxist, to socialist, to "pink." Obama himself speaks in glasnostian euphemisms that stand in for socialist rhetoric. It is a form of political "cross-dressing." Most of his cabinet, staff and "czarist" appointees speak the same "language." The press, especially if it endorses Obama's agenda, while it deals in words, either cannot fathom the double-speak, or chooses not to. Clueless or not, the mainstream news media is complicit in the success of Obama's expansion of executive and legislative powers.

Obama's academic appointees, such as Cass Sunstein, now head of the White House Office of Information and Regulatory Affairs, are hard to pin a label to unless one reads their books, speeches, and public statements, and then identifies and collates their key premises into a coherent political philosophy. That political philosophy invariably translates into socialism, or, as they prefer to call it, "progressivism," which is the saccharine, less frightening term for the same thing. They know what they are saying, and hope that most Americans do not.

Communists have a record of violently seizing power during a civil war or internal political strife. Fascists, or "national socialists," however, have a record of reaching power by stealth, exploiting a semi-free country's parliamentary structure. Hitler and his national socialists tried direct seizure of the German government in the Beer Hall Putsch, literally at the point of a gun, but failed. Hitler spent time in prison. He learned his lesson from that attempted coup and entered the "democratic" hustings. He and his party banked and built on over ten years his rhetorical skills and alleged "magnetism," both of which exploited a sheer emotionalism that smothered the irrationalism of their agenda and to which the German electorate was responsive. By 1933, Hitler and his Nazis were in power.

Were they socialists, or fascists? Communists have a habit of simply seizing private property outright. Socialists prefer to "ease" into seizure over a period of time. Fascists allow nominal private ownership of property, so long as the owners take orders from the government and cohere to its collectivist agenda. If things go wrong, the government can blame the management of a "private" company, not the policies it requires management to submit to. Both practices are usually in the name of some nationalist sentiment. Obama has capitalized on past regulatory legislation and "eased" into the banking and car manufacturing industries, and hopes to do the same with health care and insurance. Now his sights are set on the press. All this makes him a national socialist.

One of the first things the Nazis took over was the press, aided by a suspension of the Weimar Constitution. Time Magazine reported the sequence of events with an honesty foreign to most journalists today: "With the Reichstag fire as his excuse, weary old President Paul von Hindenburg signed a decree giving Chancellor Hitler & Cabinet a tyrant's powers." Of relevant interest here, given ominous actions taken by the Obama administration, and to judge by the *simpatico* political character of his appointees and staff, are particular stipulations in the German Constitution nullified by Hindenburg's decree:

> Article 118: "Every German has the right within the limits of the general laws to express his opinion by word, in writing, printing, by picture, or in any other way. . . ."
> Article 123: "All Germans have the right to gather in meetings peaceably and unarmed without announcement or particular permission. . . ."
> Article 124: "All Germans have the right to form societies or associations for purposes not contrary to the penal law.
> Article 153: "Property is safeguarded by the Constitution. . . ."

As disconnected as those "rights" were, absent an integrated philosophy of reason and individual rights, they still offered some protection. Hitler swept them from the political life of Germany like so many crumbs. That was his intention in 1923. While he was in prison dictating *Mein Kampf,* he had a very good press. But the German press barons should have taken heed of what he had to say about newspapers:

> "Freedom of the press is a nuisance that allows unpunishable lies to poison the people." (*Mein Kampf,* p. 335)

The Toledo Blade reported on September 20th that Obama met with editors from that paper and its sister paper, the Pittsburgh Post-Gazette.

> In an Oval Office interview with editors from the Pittsburgh Post-Gazette and The Blade, the President talked about the vital role journalism and newspapers play in American society. "Journalistic integrity, you know, fact-based reporting, serious investigative reporting, how to retain those ethics in all these different new media and how to make sure that it's paid for, is really a challenge," Mr. Obama said. "But it's something that I think is absolutely critical to the health of our democracy."

121

Journalistic integrity? Fact-based reporting? Serious investigative reporting? Again, Obama speaks of things about which he either knows nothing, or cares not a fig, just as he knows nothing about the Constitution he purportedly taught at the University of Chicago Law School, or cares a fig, either. But, here is his real worry:

> "I am concerned that if the direction of the news is all blogosphere, all opinions, with no serious fact-checking, no serious attempts to put stories in context, that what you will end up getting is people shouting at each other across the void but not a lot of mutual understanding,"

Just as Representative Joe Wilson shouted across a void, "You lie!"? Just as the blogosphere is compensating for the slanted, biased, non-objective reporting in the print and broadcast media, and over which the government has little or no control?

The Toledo Blade does not mention who called the meeting in the Oval Office between Obama and the editors. Did Obama summon the editors, or did the editors beg for an audience with him? The omission of this important information is a salutary instance of the shoddy state of modern journalism.

> Several bills have been introduced in Congress to aid the newspaper industry, including a Senate measure that would allow newspaper companies to restructure as nonprofits with a variety of tax breaks. The President was noncommittal about the legislation but said: "I haven't seen detailed proposals yet, but I'll be happy to look at them."

No, he hasn't seen the detailed proposals yet, but he will be happy to look at them to see if they fit into his agenda – just as he hasn't mastered the details of the health-care bills or the cap-and-trade bills and the details of any other regulatory and confiscatory legislation he would sign. The details are irrelevant to Obama. As long as the legislation regulates and confiscates, that is fine with him.

American editors and newspaper barons should also heed Hitler's annoyance with the press as they contemplate rescue by the government from their financial straits. How often has Obama inveighed against the "lies," "distortions," and "fishy" information that have appeared in newspapers over the last year? How often has he criticized the right of assembly exercised by Americans to protest his health-care and other coercive legislation, and called such Americans dupes of those lies and distortions? How often has he expressed anger over any degree of opposition to his agenda, an opposition which, whether frank and open or watered down and euphemized in the press, is based on statements and allegations appearing in the press?

Obama cannot but believe that freedom of the press is also a nuisance, that the people have been "poisoned" by it to oppose his agenda, and that the "lies" on which that opposition is founded ought to be punished. (He has hired Cass Sunstein to devise punishment.) How else to explain the opposition, he must ask himself. How could there be any ideology other than his own? Leftist ideology is not so much embedded in him, as he is embedded in it. He sees this country and the world through the prisms of Marx and Alinsky. As his ideology has been propagated and promoted by the Democratic National Committee, with millions of dollars in assistance from organizations such as MoveOn, he cannot imagine that resistance to his agenda could be anything but organized by a coalition of Republicans, "racists," and other conspiratorial ogres; that is, he cannot imagine that a large segment of the American population could object to his agenda and ideology and establish their own "correspondence committees" to express their opposition, without any political or moral guidance from the Republicans.

Obama's idea of a "free press" is to appear on popular talk shows and news analysis programs whose hosts he can count on not to pose questions of any substance. In those public venues, on the White House lawn, in staged press conferences, on the Internet, he is free to spout his agenda and assurances. But he and his handlers (principally Rahm Emanuel, chief of staff) will not brook any back-talk or probing queries. Representative Joe Wilson's "You lie!" must have shaken him more than either he or his staff of ventriloquists, marionettes and dissemblers will admit. Wilson's statement was, after all, a truth spoken before a national audience; it exposed a core tactic permissible in practical leftist politics – that lies are a weapon as a means to the acquisition of power, just as *taqiyya* is a form of Islamic religious dissimulation, by which falsehoods and concealment aimed against non-Muslims are approved by the Koran as a legitimate form of *jihad*.

The mainstream news media, which includes such periodicals as The New York Times and The Washington Post, and also the three major television networks, would not mind a co-opting by the federal government, as long as the expropriation (and the surrender) was promoted as an "efficiency" or "consolidation" move, *a la* Goebbels, and as long as the various entities retained some nominal independence, but reorganized, according to the proposed agenda, as non-profit organizations. What they choose to advocate, endorse and support now – which is Obama's agenda – would become an obligation.

This leaves Fox News, for the moment, as the Will Kane of the news media, virtually alone in the media in taking on the vengeance-on-America Frank Miller gang of the White House and Congress. Never mind the irony that both conservatives and leftists once claimed *High Noon* as an allegory (or "metaphor') for their specific politics. The difference now is that the townsmen are also rallying to protect themselves and their freedom from the Obama gang – and that gang is socialist in purpose, fascist in practice.

The townsmen are receiving no help from the mainstream news media. The Obama gang they rightly fear and will fight. The MSM they despise.

September 2009

Speechless Speech

"I'm not a bigot. You know the kind of books I've written about the Civil Rights movement in this country," Williams said on the show. "But when I get on a plane, I got to tell you, if I see people who are in Muslim garb and I think, you know, they are identifying themselves first and foremost as Muslims, I get worried. I get nervous."

So said Juan Williams, news analyst for National Public Radio (NPR), to Bill O'Reilly on Fox News. The remark got him promptly fired from NPR, and subsequently hired fulltime by Fox News. What was NPR's reasoning?

His remarks on *The O'Reilly Factor* this past Monday were inconsistent with our editorial standards and practices, and undermined his credibility as a news analyst with NPR," the statement read.

And what editorial standards and practices might those be? No one really knows, but it is easy to guess, to judge by the wholly left-liberal-progressive bias and content of all its news programming. From NPR's perspective, Williams not only shot from the hip, but shot himself in the foot. Williams expressed a private concern shared by multitudes of Americans, including very likely many denizens of NPR, when they see Muslims in their tribal garb anywhere, and not just in airports. But those other NPR employees will not be punished, because they have kept their mouths shut.

Using Williams's pseudo-gaffe as an example, Gary Wickert, an insurance trial lawyer in Wisconsin and author or editor of several books on insurance, wrote an interesting article on Pajamas Media on the corrosive effects of political correctness, "Political Correctness and the Thought Police" (November 1st). He begins by stating that political correctness is hard to define.

It's hard to define political correctness, but like pornography, you know it when you see it. Some say it is a social philosophy that strives to ensure nobody will ever be offended by anything, ever. Wikipedia defines it as a term which "denotes language, ideas, policies, and behavior seen as seeking to minimize social and institutional offense in occupational, gender, racial, cultural, sexual orientation, disability, and age-related contexts." Merriam-Webster defines it as "conforming to a belief that language and practices which could offend political sensibilities — as in matters of sex or race — should be eliminated."

Two minor errors in the piece should be corrected: Mr. Wickert says that "niggardly" (a supposedly offensive term discussed in the article) means "spendthrift." Actually, it means not quite the opposite: "ungenerous," or "cheap," or "penny-wise." Then, he invented a new term, "cow-tow," when he meant "kowtow."

However, his article delves handily but inconsistently into the causes and consequences of political correctness in speech, action and policy.

I penned a review of *Guidelines for Bias-Free Writing*, published by The Task Force on Bias-Free Language, in 1996 for The Social Critic, "The Ghouls of Grammatical Egalitarianism."

> Thought orthodoxy is not synonymous with thought control. There is no Federal Board of Language Usage to which publishers must submit their books and journals to be tested for discriminatory or disparaging language before they can be put on the market for sale to the public. However, while no official agency of control exists, there is a kind of interlocking directorate of semi-public institutions and organizations which accomplishes the same purpose by presenting a united front against freedom of expression and imposing orthodoxy on our culture's intellectual and literary pacesetters. 'Say what you please, we're not censors!....But say it our way, or do not bother to say it.'

> Short of overt government repression, I cannot imagine a more insidious form of thought control than this, which is to thrust independent minds of whatever professional suasion or degree of ability into a purgatory that is not quite freedom and not quite slavery.

(See also my entry, "Censorship," in *The Encyclopedia of Library and Information Science*.)

The Task Force was created by the Association of American University Presses (the AAUP, see its membership here) in response to constant mewlings from other cultural quarters to research and write *Guidelines*, which has become a kind of *Psalter of Bowdleristic Banter* for academics and others obsessively sensitive to sensitivity.

Only H.L. Mencken could do better than P.J. O'Rourke, who reviewed this abomination in August 1995:

> The pharisaical, malefic, and incogitant *Guidelines for Bias-Free Writing* is a product of the pointy-headed wowsers at the Association of American University Presses, seven women, two men] who established a Task Force on Bias-Free Language filled with cranks, pokenoses, blowhards, four-flushers, and pettifogs.

This foolish and contemptible product of years wasted in mining the shafts of indignation has been published by the cow-besieged, basketball-sotted sleep-away camp for hick bourgeois offspring, Indiana University, under the aegis of its University Press, a traditional dumping ground for academic deadwood so bereft of talent, intelligence, and endeavor as to be useless even in the full precincts of Midwestern state college classrooms.

Politically correct speech and writing are not necessarily traceable, as Wickert alleges, to the Frankfurt School and Marxism, although the two are closely allied ideologically. I doubt that even David Axelrod, Cass Sunstein, or Anita Dunn would claim that politically correct speech is Communist in origin, though they would have no problem enforcing it. Politically correct speech in America, as a phenomenon, is a direct result of legislated envy.

Politically correct speech is the political bowdlerizing of thought and expression of thought. It requires ceaseless "conditioning" by government- and academically-approved wardens. As Thomas Bowdler sought to expunge "indecencies" from language by simply removing them from literary works (such as Shakespeare's plays), politically correct speech seeks to expunge objectionable terms from the mind. The "authorities" plant *un bacio della morte* on unwelcome terms, as surely as Michael Corleone condemned his brother Fredo in *Godfather II.*

However, while a mind cannot be forced, it can be corrupted. That is the sole purpose of politically correct speech. A corrupted mind will accede to anything. It is ready to be moulded and given its marching orders.

Political correctness is an insidious, poliomyelitic epistemological affliction that attacks, not the brainstem or spinal cord, but language, concepts, and ideas in one's mind to render the mind an impotent and helpless plaything of authorities or the thought police. In short, it attacks the mind, and, like Orwell's Newspeak Dictionary in *Nineteen Eighty-Four*, seeks to reduce the range of the mind by homogenizing and cleansing its contents and imposing a literal mindless conformity.

The catch is that, while imbeciles would not know the difference between plain, politically correct, and "incorrect" speech – they are not the objects of the tyranny, it is only active minds that are the object of controls – it works only if one is willing to submit, Muslim-style, to a higher "authority," only if one knows that one is expected to knuckle under and bow to the god of sensitivity.

Compliance with politically correct speech, however, is voluntary. It is a conscious action requiring knowledge of what one is submitting to and for what reason, and knowledge of what one is abandoning. This in turn contributes to a deadening miasma of habitual, congenital conformity in politics, art, speech, and other realms of endeavor, even in soccer moms who applaud scoreless, "non-competitive" games – designed to protect the feelings of the losers and bolster their "self-esteem" – which in turn contributes to the growth of a servile, passive, complacent citizenry.

And a dishonest one, as well, for while "incorrect" terms may be suppressed, the banished terms form a black market of expression. They do not disappear. Genuinely offensive terms, which would not be employed by a civil person in any circumstance, such as *wetback, Polack, wop*, or *kike* take on even more vicious meanings, as well as prejudice-free terms such as *black, idiot, moron*, and *imbecile.* (Note: *Black* basically means either a color or an absence of color; the latter three terms were formerly clinical terms used to measure thinking or reasoning capacity, and are now "disused." I have no idea what terms have replaced them, except the popular, universally applicable and now humorously denigrating *challenged.*)

In the written realm, political correctness results in staleness of writing, in thinking, in literature. It is not a power exercised with the arrogance of breaking down one's front door. It sneaks in through the back door and insinuates itself in one's daily life.

It is only government force that can fuel and sustain political correctness by imposing penalties on incorrectness. The trials of Geert Wilders in the Netherlands, of Elisabeth Sabaditsch-Wolfe in Austria, and of columnist Mark Steyn in Canada are proof of that power, a power handed government by its allies in academia. Political correctness is a trickle-down phenomenon with dual ends: the punishment and fettering of independent minds; and fostering the increase in truncated minds, which are more easily managed, manipulated, and led. It is a communicable polio that corrupts an increasing number of fields, from the military to politics to education and art. It is an enfeebling disease, promoted and imposed by government.

Political correctness, especially in speech, vitiates a person's epistemology, with the consequence of creating a universal state of desideratum, or the nagging sense that the identifying terms of some things have been deliberately banished or eradicated. One's only option is to conform to an arbitrarily enforced norm. For an individual who knows the terms, it puts him on a cautious self-defense regime that is more destructive repression than it is studied discretion.

It is noteworthy that it is specially protected or patronized groups that are the beneficiaries of politically correct speech. They are viewed in the same way that certain animals and plants have been designated "endangered species." They beg protection from indiscriminate speech or "wounding words" and real and imagined insults. The disabled, the aged, the mentally incapable, and so on are allied in a unique menagerie of untouchables and the socially coddled, and safe-housed in the same iron-clad fortress of exclusivity with the spotted owl and the delta smelt and, more recently, Muslims.

To echo Juan Williams, whenever I encounter politically correct speech and action, I get worried and nervous. It means that I am dealing with dishonesty, with corruption, with a consciously shrunken mind that demands that I speak and write on its terms.

But then, as a free man, I simply laugh and say what I wish.

November 2010

The Censors' Cabal

It is a whispering campaign to counter the harmful – shall we say "hateful"? – effects of freedom of speech and the liberty of inquiry. To whom are they harmful and hateful? To President Barack Obama. To his administration. To Congress. To tribal "communities" of every stripe. They know that the truth is out there, about them, about their actions, about their motives, and it must be suppressed. – albeit without saying that it is being censored.

The first evidence of Obama's true intentions was the overt but clumsy invitation to Americans last summer to report via email to the White House any "fishy" anti-administration talk by other Americans. Obama received a stinging, well-deserved rebuke, one delivered chiefly in the Internet's blogosphere and which spread like slow molasses to the mainstream media, which did not welcome a rebuke of their copacetic favorite and sometime messiah. The White House's "rat-on-your-neighbor" site was taken down, but not before first crashing under the weight of countless thousands of retorts from Americans to Obama to mind his own business.

But Obama and Company haven't given up. They and Congress believe their "business" is to "run" the country, and that includes filtering and censoring what Americans read, think, and say. Like Muslims who object to images of Mohammed, their feelings are hurt and their sensibilities offended by criticism and caricature. Negative portrayals of Obama and his administration and his ilk in Congress are considered to be abrasive and secularly "blasphemous." Obama's "approval ratings" are plummeting and Congress's promise to shatter the floor. It's all the fault of the First Amendment. It must be emasculated, qualified, and delegitimitized.

Their ideological clones in the Federal Communications Commission (FCC) and Federal Trade Commission (FTC) are assiduously searching for a means to impose censorship without calling it censorship. They are moved by a fear that the Tea Parties and an indiscriminate and unobstructed access to news other than what is reported by the MSM have demonstrated a power that threatens the hegemony of collectivism. They wish to silence anyone and everyone who pursues and exposes the truth.

The FTC is casting about for the means to "save" journalism, that is, the journalism it approves of. That is, the Commission is searching for a justification for meddling. It concedes that Internet journalism exists, but by implication discounts it as "true" journalism. After all, it isn't regulated or subsidized by the government; ergo, its news is highly suspect. What it wishes to do is find a way to bolster "traditional" news coverage and reportage, whatever that may be, for the concept is nowhere defined in its draft report.

They want a captive, obedient electorate as dumbed down and indoctrinated exclusively by government-approved news and government-vetted "journalists," as hapless and helpless as school children instructed in the ways of Islam and the environment and "Native American" culture, while fed miniscule portions of Howard Zinn-style American history that guarantee children will grow up to be subservient tax-cows and "good," selfless citizens.

One of those means is to tax the blogosphere and force it to subsidize its competitors. Another is to establish a "public fund" to subsidize newspapers, other approved media, and journalists by taxing the broadcast spectrum, consumer electronics, commercial advertising, and cell phone ISPs. Still another is to rewrite IRS rules to better protect newspapers and broadcast stations from the Internet. Nine pages of *The Federal Trade Commission Staff Discussion Draft of Potential Policy Recommendations to Support the Reinvention of Journalism* (the *Draft*) are devoted to how the IRS can further perpetuate "traditional" journalism (pp. 21-29).

Indeed, the IRS plays a heavy-handed role in what may be defined as public interest-oriented news and mere "commercial" news. If The New York Times, for example, claims that it is chiefly a "public service" and can prove it caters to the "public interest," while its editorializing is just a sideline, then it qualifies for tax exemptions or credits (in other words, a subsidy or tax break enjoyed by few other papers). If a newspaper's chief purpose is to promulgate an ideology and is not published by a certified non-profit organization (and it's the IRS that decides what is a "non-profit" organization), then it gets no exemptions or credits.

The FTC *Draft* is essentially a 47-page excursion into fantasy land. Journalism has already "reinvented" itself without any government support. How many newspapers, for example, *do not* now have free or advertiser-paid or subscriber-paid online daily editions? The only "support" the government can legitimately provide is to stay out of it.

The FTC staff discussions, however, created a smorgasbord of policy options to recommend (to whom? Congress? The White House? Cass Sunstein? Henry Waxman?). All of them require government action. Defenders of government action make the specious claim that the government has always been involved in promoting journalism and newspapers.

Besides, the *Draft* assures the public, the report only seeks

to prompt discussion of whether to recommend policy changes to support the ongoing "reinvention" of journalism, and, if so, which specific proposals appear most useful, feasible, platform-neutral, resistant to bias, and unlikely to cause unintended consequences in addressing emerging gaps in news coverage.

The FTC has only discussed "suggestions," not concrete plans of action.

"These are nothing more or less than information gathering meetings," says FTC spokesman Peter Kaplan, who adds that the agency has no current plans other than to publish the hearing results this fall. Beyond that, points out Lisa Graves, executive director of the Center for Media and Democracy, protestations aside, government has played a role in encouraging a healthy press from the dawn of the republic.

"First, we had an ink subsidy and then we had a postal subsidy both of which helped a free press to flourish," she says.

Yes, Miss Graves, the government played a role in encouraging the press – by largely not meddling in it except for the "ink subsidy" and the postal subsidy. (I could find no reference anywhere about an "ink subsidy," unless Graves was referring to a tax break on printer's ink purchases or to a tariff or excise tax break on its importation.)

Much of the *Draft* seems heavily influenced by the findings and recommendations of a USC/Annenberg School for Communication and Journalism study, "Public Policy and Funding the News." It claims that the Internet and its blogging news reporters have benefited from government investment in development of the Internet, and will benefit again from TARPs I and II.

Long before the United States was founded, the Postal Service was subsidizing the news business. It was in good measure the free-mailing privileges conferred by many postmasters that allowed a robust network of colonial newspapers to emerge. George Washington wanted all newspapers, in fact, to have 100 percent subsidized mailing costs. The Postal Act of 1792 rejected the idea of a total subsidy, but it codified highly subsidized and extremely low rates. What brought a halt to publishers' receiving 75 percent discounts on their mailed news products was the financial crisis that engulfed the Postal Service in the late 1960s.(p. 11) (*Italics* mine.)

These are some of the transparent rationalizations that seek to sanction "public funding" of newspapers, the broadcast spectrum, and the Internet. I italicized the first sentence of this vacuous rationalization because the "Postal Service" could not have predated the country's founding. There was indeed a British Crown-controlled postal "service" but its purpose was not to foster the growth of colonial newspapers. See the USPS site for clarification of the purpose of the Crown and post-Revolutionary postal services, and Benjamin Franklin's role in them. And for a history of the development of the Internet and the government's role in its initial role as a tool of national defense (it did little to develop the commercial potential), go here.

It does not follow that if, historically, government had *some* role in the growth of news communications, it should "monitor" the "reinvention" of it by taking control of it.

The Annenberg study offers recommendations as woozy and ill-defined as those in the *Draft*.

> As policymakers debate how to respond to the fast decline of the news business, we offer the following principles as guidance:
>
> • First and foremost, do no harm. A cycle of powerful innovation is under way. To
> the extent possible, government should avoid retarding the emergence of new models of news-gathering.
>
> • Second, the government should help promote innovation, as it did when the Department of Defense funded the research that created the Internet or when NASA funded the creation of satellites that made cable TV and direct radio and TV possible.
>
> • Third, for commercial media, government-supported mechanisms that are content neutral – such as copyright protections, postal subsidies and taxes – are preferable to those that call upon the government to fund specific news outlets, publications or programs. However policymakers proceed, they should do so based on facts rather than myths. The government has always supported the commercial news business. It does so today. Unless the government takes affirmative action, though, the level of support is almost certain to decline at this important time in the history of journalism. (p. 16)

In short, the study does not question a government role in journalism. It does not specifically oppose regulation of any media. It makes ambiguous suggestions that government "do no harm." It seems to say: Wait until someone has a brilliant idea and a developed innovation; then you can jump in and control it for the "public good." Whether or not that would be "doing harm" will be just someone's subjective opinion. The "public interest" comes first.

The FCC is more obviously out to control speech, that is, to prohibit speech it deems offensive, specifically "hate speech." But, as one blogger pointed out, the protection of "hate speech" is what the First Amendment is all about. No one has ever taken exception to "love speech" or demanded that it be censored.

The FCC is mulling over the petition of a collection of various collectivist groups, the "National Hispanic Media Coalition" (NHMC), to "monitor" speech on the radio and on the Internet, with a "view" to regulating its content and intent. But, to regulate or banish "hate speech" – whose ever definition of the term it may be – is to regulate or banish all speech.

NMHC's Petition urges the Commission to examine the extent and effects of hate speech in media, including the likely link between hate speech and hate crimes, and to explore non-regulatory ways to counteract its negative impacts. As NHMC has awaited Commission action, hate, extremism and misinformation have been on the rise, and even more so in the past week as the media has focused on Arizona's passage of one of the one of the harshest pieces of anti-Latino in this country's history, SB1070.

There are forty-one more references to "hate speech" in the petition, the *Future of Media and Information Needs of Communities in a Digital Age*, while the phrase "hate, extremism and misinformation" appears four times. SB1070, however, is merely a replicant of the U.S. law, which remains haphazardly enforced. Again, nowhere in the petition are *hate speech* and *misinformation* defined. Their meanings are up for grabs by the most vocal and "victimized" communities (read tribes, groups, gangs).

And, there is no "non-regulatory way" to "counteract" any speech, hateful or not, not without the use of government force. "Counteraction" means action, which means *force*, which can be either withholding a radio station's license, or pressure put on a station's sponsors, or just Hugo Chavez's thuggish way of "counteracting" hate speech.

If "hate speech" is protected by the First Amendment, the recent Helen Thomas episode has demonstrated one of the practical values of that Amendment: it allows individuals to reveal their philosophy, their morality, and their souls for all to see. One may agree with them, disagree with them, or ignore them.

But, readers, viewers, and listeners should keep this in mind if they see anything benign in government regulation of speech: One of its purposes is to rig the airwaves, newspapers, television, and the Internet so that one *cannot* ignore its own propaganda, or know any truth but what the government says it is. How would one be able to judge or determine the truth? That would entail thinking, which is precisely what the government doesn't want anyone to do. Just believe, and obey.

> "Intellectual freedom cannot exist without political freedom," wrote Ayn Rand. "Political freedom cannot exist without economic freedom; a free mind and a free market are *corollaries.*"*

The current administration has made clear its attacks on intellectual freedom, political freedom, and economic freedom.

An attack on one has always implicitly meant an attack on the other two. This is what those who would defend the First Amendment must also understand. They must grasp that indivisible integration of freedoms. One cannot uphold freedom of speech to the exclusion of the other preconditions of it, as liberals have done for over a century, which is uphold freedom of speech while advocating the seizure or control of property. Logical consistency required that they now attack what they once defended. Their more ideologically consistent and activist brethren on the Left are only too happy to oblige.

*"For the New Intellectual," in *For the New Intellectual* (1961). New York: Signet/Penguin Books, p. 25.

June 2010

The Logical End of Politically Correct Speech

"It is not so curious that in the wake of the Danish cartoon conflict, during which the American press and news media revealed their tepid commitment to freedom of speech and the inviolacy of the First Amendment, incidents of assaults on that freedom would not only multiply, but assume odd but no less ominous forms."

That was how I opened a commentary on the corruptive power of politically correct speech in "Moving Towards Freedomless Speech" on this site in May 2006. I further remarked:

> "To return to thought control: The 'control' that enforces 'orthodoxy' in speech by individuals is simply fear of retribution, reprisal, or financial and personal ruin. To work, thought or speech control relies exclusively on self-censorship. The instances of operable thought control are as ubiquitous and innocuous in our culture as countless drops of water falling on one's forehead in a Chinese torture."

And,

> "On a fundamental cultural level, it is no coincidence that the introduction and gradual acceptance of the concept of 'hate crimes' paralleled the stealthy and de facto imposition of politically correct speech. Politically correct speech, in turn, has established the grounds for punishable 'tactless language.'"

Politically correct speech, we are seeing, inevitably leads to politically correct thought, if the speech is not flouted, opposed, or corrected. Who can enforce that epistemology-wrecking and metaphysics-warping nomenclature? Who can enforce mental blank-outs?

Inevitably, government force. But our federal and state governments have not yet imposed censorship. They are evading that damning label – the term still carries an onus of tyranny that its advocates avoid like primitive savages, even though it is tyranny they wish to impose – by stealthily coming in through the backdoors of speech codes, vocabularies of "sensitivity," campaign finance laws, and the like. No, they are allowing the gauleiters of correct speech to lay the groundwork for censorship in numerous fields of thought and action.

The latest casualties in freedom of thought and speech in the name of orthodoxy may be science and scientists. The Daily Telegraph (London) of March 12th featured this disturbing article, under the headline, "Scientists threatened for 'climate denial'":

"Scientists who questioned mankind's impact on climate change have received death threats and claim to have been shunned by the scientific community.

"They say the debate on global warming has been 'hijacked' by a powerful alliance of politicians, scientists and environmentalists who have stifled all questioning about the true environmental impact of carbon dioxide emissions.

"Timothy Ball, a former climatology professor at the University of Winnipeg in Canada, has received five death threats by email since raising concerns about the degree to which man was affecting climate change. One of the emails warned that, if he continued to speak out, he would not live to see further global warming."

What is the next step after threats to enforce *goodthink* in a semi-free society? Outright force, as we witnessed when homicidal anti-abortionists took shots at doctors, terrorized women seeking abortions, and firebombed abortion clinics.

"Last week," the Daily Telegraph article continued, "Professor Ball appeared in The Great Global Warming Swindle…a documentary in which several scientists claimed the theory of man-made global warming had become a 'religion,' forcing alternative explanations to be ignored."

Yes, environmentalism is a religion, although it didn't just recently become one. It has been a religion – a system of reason-proof intrinsic values that places nature far above man's survival – ever since the first savages sacrificed one of their own to placate the mysterious moods of gods. Reality, facts, evidence, and proofs have never stood in the way of faith in the incomprehensible.

"Richard Lindzen, the professor of Atmospheric Science at Massachusetts Institute of Technology – who also appeared on the documentary – recently claimed: 'Scientists who dissent from the alarmism have seen their funds disappear, their work derided, and themselves labeled as industry stooges. Consequently, lies about climate change gain credence even when they fly in the face of science.'"

Another scientist on the program stated, "The Green movement has hijacked the issue of climate change. It is ludicrous to suggest the only way to deal with the problem is to start micro-managing everyone, which is what environmentalists seem to want to do."

Premise check here: Climate change, or global warming, is not a "problem." And that scientist errs in another premise, that environmentalists wish to micro-manage everyone (as totalitarians are wont to do), presumably for their own good and the good of the earth. If he examined the Green movement as closely as he might data from a sample ice core from the Arctic or Antarctic, he would conclude that environmentalists wish to micro-manage man out of existence – first with solar and wind power, then with ethanol, then with florescent light bulbs, and God knows what other "energy-conserving," "environment friendly" doodads and scams someone or some group might foist on a defenseless public.

What the environmentalists do not wish to hear – nor wish anyone else to hear – are some of the conclusions and observations of the scientists who appeared on the Great Global Warming Swindle program: that if there is warming, it is caused by sunspot activity, which drives up CO_2 levels, which may or may not mean anything; that the environmental movement is driven by politics; and that scientists who question or deny the "truth" that man is causing the rise of CO_2 levels find their names appended to international reports that endorse the man-made global warming mantra. That is consistent with the style of environmentalists: threats of force, preceded by fraud and forgery.

What about those polar bears clinging to melting icebergs as they drift into the ocean (and often landing in Iceland, where they are shot)? Another Daily Telegraph article from March 9th, "Polar bears 'thriving as the Arctic warms up'," among other things reports a rise in the polar bear population.

> "Polar bear experts said that numbers had increased not because of climate change but due to the efforts of conservationists. The battle to ban the hunting of Harp seal pups has meant the seal population has soared – boosting the bears' food supply. At the same time, fewer seal hunters are around to hunt bears."

But those poor bears, hanging ten on shrinking ice cubes! Said one professor from the University of Alberta about "a celebrated photograph of a bear and its cub floating on a tiny iceberg, the animals often travel in that way. 'Bears will often hang out on glacier ice or large pieces of multi-year ice.'"

Last week a biologist on a San Francisco radio program raised the point that since polar bears are a species closely related to grizzly bears, both species carnivores, they have no problem hunting on land and finding food that way.

"Tina Cummings, a biologist attached to the Alaskan government, questioned whether they needed sea ice to survive, saying they could adapt to hunt on land and find alternative food sources to seals."

So, it isn't just Muslims who object to freedom of speech and the "inconvenient" truths about Islam such freedom might reveal. The fire and brimstone faithful of another religion, environmentalism, also wish to squelch anyone who questions the soundness or truthfulness of their "science" of global warming and man's contribution to it.

"Slay them wherever you find them," orders the Koran about infidels and unbelievers. "Call them names, accuse them of denial, of trafficking with the capitalist Satan, of using tactless or insensitive language, shun them," order the environmentalist gurus. And if the unbelievers won't shut up, threaten them with death.

When men begin to resort to death threats and *ad hominem* arguments as means of persuasion, then one should know immediately that a fraud is being perpetrated and that the facts of reality are not on their side. To submit to such persuasion is to submit to thought control, which can "work" only if one vanquishes one's own mind. A mind cannot be forced, said Ayn Rand's John Galt; it can only abdicate.

March 2007

Nike of Samothrace, The Louvre, Paris

Culture

Humor Me

As a change of pace, I would like to respond to or rebut some reader comments made about a trio of movies mentioned in "A "Mess of Pottage" (November 24) on the Rule of Reason site, particularly about *The Manchurian Candidate* and *His Girl Friday*. President-elect Barack Obama and his plan to expand FDR's welfare state programs, together with the looming threats of Islam, Russia and other predators, including Congress, are not going away any time soon, so there will be plenty of time and opportunity to discuss them in the future.

Some readers agreed with my very brief endorsement of *The Manchurian Candidate*. It is a very serious, revealing, and compelling drama. But, believe it or not, some critics treated it as a comedy or satire! I can only surmise that these critics' intention was to deny the seriousness of the story and infect the minds of anyone who saw it soon after its release. Virtually the sole humor in it is expressed by one of the villains, Yen Lo (played by Khigh Dhiegh), the apparent mastermind behind the Sino-Soviet plot to install a president in the White House who could help facilitate the Communist conquest of the United States. This humor attacks the U.S. and Lo's immediate victims, and is not funny. But, in the context of the story, Lo's humor plays a legitimate role. It underscores his and his co-conspirators' evil, much as Ellsworth Toohey's humor underscores his evil in Ayn Rand's *The Fountainhead*.

My only reservation about the film is that it credits evil men with too much intelligence or with a species of omniscience, that is, with a capacity for successful long-range planning or with the ability to make the *unreal* appear to be real. Recall, for example, those notoriously failed Five-Year Plans, and our own government's actions to "fine-tune" or "manage" the economy, a policy failure which it refuses to acknowledge and which Obama plans to exacerbate with his own Lenin-esque New Economic Policy.

It seems that two readers of the "Pottage" commentary have based their objections to the humor in *His Girl Friday* on what very little Rand wrote or spoke about humor. While she addressed or identified some fundamentals concerning humor, I do not think she exhausted the subject, perhaps having had little time or interest to devote to it. She did remark, however, that

> "Humor is a metaphysical negation. We regard as funny that which contradicts reality: the incongruous and the grotesque."*

And,

> "What you find funny depends on what you want to negate. It is proper to laugh at evil (the literary form of which is satire) or at the negligible. But to laugh at the good is vicious."**

Rand wrote what I would say were general guidelines to humor, and sketched out the parameters of what is legitimate and vicious humor. There may be in the Rand archives at ARI as-yet unpublished material on the subject. I am reminded of the plot of *The Name of the Rose* (1986), set in a medieval monastery about a lost book or treatise by Aristotle on comedy (with Sean Connery as the detective monk).

Some comedies are funny, other comedies not so funny, and still others not funny at all. *His Girl Friday* (1940) is uproariously funny. It does not rely on sight gags or humor as crude as that of The Three Stooges or even of the Marx Brothers. Its humor is just a shade above subtle, and pokes fun at the metaphysically negligible, such as Rosalind Russell's fiancé and the Mayor and his lackey sheriff. This was the second film version of the 1931 production, and far superior to it. It was based on the play co-written by Ben Hecht and Charles MacArthur (1928), who also collaborated on the screenplay of another "screwball" comedy, *Twentieth Century* (1934), and on three non-comedic dramas: *Spellbound* (1945), *Notorious* (1946), and *Gunga Din* (1939).

The central story line of *His Girl Friday* is the hilariously unscrupulous campaign waged by Walter Burns (Cary Grant), the editor-in-chief, to keep his best reporter, Hildy Johnson (Russell), from leaving his newspaper and his life. (In the original play and first film version, Hildy was a male role, and no romantic relationship between Burns and Hildy was suggested or insinuated). Burns entertains no dichotomy between his paper and Hildy; they are one and the same, and he is in love with them both. Of course, all the actions Burns takes to keep Hildy are exaggerations of actions that could be taken in real life: setting up Hildy's insurance salesman fiancé for several falls, beating other newspapers to a breaking story, getting the goods on a pompous, two-faced politician and his cronies.

As for Hildy, she is tempted to leave the career of a "newspaperman" (that's what she calls herself) for the sedate existence of a housewife ("…and in Albany, too," Burns kids her), and possibly because her romance with Burns hasn't progressed beyond chasing the news together and the occasional bedroom fling.

Burns and Hildy are divorced, but the divorce isn't working (now, *that's* funny). Burns knows Hildy better than Hildy knows herself, and it doesn't take long for him to convince her that Bruce Baldwin (played wonderfully down to the meanest mannerism by Ralph Bellamy) is not the man for her and that the conventional life Bruce promises her would be suffocatingly dull.

Burns succeeds in keeping Hildy. She is a value to him. That makes him, if not the hero of an epic, then the hero of a satire on newspapers. "Screwball" comedy like *His Girl Friday* is not supposed to be taken seriously. It is a kind of dessert to be enjoyed after a main course. Both Rule of Reason commentators implied that since the film did not adhere to the defining attributes of an epic or serious drama, then it couldn't be good. No one is supposed to take seriously the *bête noire* of the story, the pathetically meek and unstable Earl Williams, scheduled to be executed for shooting a policeman but whose timely pardon by the governor is suppressed by the corrupt mayor. He escapes in the most ludicrous circumstances and winds up hiding in a roll-top desk. Another commentator asked,

"How can you laugh at a woman convincing a murderer that it isn't his fault that he used a gun to kill a man because, after all, the purpose of a gun is to kill?"

In this instance, one can't. Hildy, in the prison interview scene, isn't trying to convince Williams that it wasn't his fault; she is simply probing the mind of a lunatic to find a context in which to write her story, and in the bargain mocking Marxist economics (production for use, not for profit, etc.). And, one doesn't laugh *at* Hildy; one merely appreciates her sense of a news story and the lengths to which she will pursue it. So, one laughs *with* her as she pursues it, such as when she literally tackles the bailiff who can grant her the prison interview with Earl Williams.

What is also humorous is Hildy's futile efforts to combat Walter Burns' constant scheming to stymie her impending marriage to Bruce Baldwin. She is foiled by him everywhere she turns. By the film's end, she is furiously pounding out the story on her typewriter, taking her cues from Walter Burns, while Bruce is on the far periphery of her consciousness, contradictory to her character and rendered negligible. She is at home, and Walter Burns has won.

His Girl Friday is one of my favorite comedies. Each line of dialogue in it feeds the next at a nonstop pace; it is the dialogue that establishes the context for the action, instead of the other way around, which is the standard practice in most comedy. It is from this and other films (not all comedies, of course, not to mention plays and novels) that I learned how to craft dialogue for my own stories.

Rand wrote,

"Good natured, charming humor is never directed at a value, but always at the undesirable or negligible. It has the result of confirming values; if you laugh at the contradictory or pretentious, you are in that act confirming the real or valuable."***

That statement can apply to much of what could be called benevolent comedy. A comedy can feature admirable, eccentric, or likeable characters caught in preposterous or absurd situations. American instances of this in film are *Bringing Up Baby* (1938), *The Philadelphia Story* (1940), *Ball of Fire* (1941), and *Born Yesterday* (1950). British instances are *The Importance of Being Earnest* (1952), *The Lavender Hill Mob* (1951), and The *Man in the White Suit* (1952). There are many more instances of this level of comedy in film, too numerous to mention here.

Humor – the benevolent, non-vicious kind, at least – also is highly contextual. Someone who might enjoy the television series *Fawlty Towers* may be left cold by *My Name is Earl*; conversely, someone whose measure of good comedy is *The King of Queens* may be unmoved by *P.G. Wodehouse Theatre*. The context and what enjoyment one derives from any of these television series, or any comedy, both depend on one's sense of life: Is it benevolent and rational, or malevolent and eclectically chaotic?

Does a person need a laugh track to prompt him that something funny has happened or has been said? Should a comedy require a person's full focus to detect, appreciate or evaluate its humor, or should it patronize his mental passivity? Does one enjoy seeing a good character get his "comeuppance," or a bad
character his? Is one willing to suspend belief in order to enjoy a light-hearted, benevolent comedy, or should one emulate the Classicists, and approach it in a second-hand, doctrinaire frame of mind?

If Aristotle truly wrote a treatise on comedy as a companion or supplement to his *Poetics*, these and other questions might have been answered. Except for plot, characterization, and resolution, the requisites for great drama are not all applicable to comedy. Drama is the broader literary form and subsumes all the criteria necessary for good comedy. Some of the greatest literature also includes unparalleled humor.

What did not amuse Queen Victoria might have amused me.

*Chapter 11, "Special Forms of Literature," in *Ayn Rand – The Art of Fiction: A Guide for Writers and Readers*, edited by Tore Boeckmann, Plume softcover, 2000, p. 165.
**Ibid, p. 166
***Ibid, p. 166

November 2008

H.L. Mencken, *Au Contraire*

"So far as I can make out, I believe in only one thing: liberty."
—Henry L. Mencken to Ernest Boyd, 1925

It is rare any more that I do not feel compelled to address the rise of statism in this country, abetted as it is by the Millionaire Mendicants of Capitol Hill, the Mooners of Mecca, or the Mariachi Marauders of the Southwest. Not to mention the Ground Zero Gang. One of the most astute, devastating, and frequently amusing observers of American politics and culture was Henry L. Mencken (1880-1956). His "talent to amuse" is never pointless or irrelevant to the subjects of his scrutiny. It is always employed to make a point. The "Sage of Baltimore" once quipped, "The urge to save humanity is almost always only a false-face for the urge to rule it." How true. Look to Washington, or any state capital.

I enjoy his journalistic style, which is consistently infused with acerbic wit and benign contempt. It is rarely vitriolic or bitter. And I concur with most of his observations, most of which still ricochet today with embarrassing veracity. I have not been able to find an exception to that rule. As a keen auditor of human behavior, he dealt in timeless universals and verities. One wonders what he would have to say about the likes of President Barack Obama, Nancy Pelosi, Joe Biden, Rahm Emanuel, and that whole, altruistically ambitious gang. They are, after all, moved by the urge to save America, even if it means ruling it. And they have demonstrated that they do want to rule. Regimes rule. Republics govern.

No President was immune from his mordant pen. Here is what he wrote in 1921 about President Warren J. Harding's speeches:

> He writes the worst English that I have ever encountered. It reminds me of a string of wet sponges; it reminds me of tattered washing on the line; it reminds me of stale bean soup, of college yells, of dogs barking idiotically through endless nights. It is so bad that a sort of grandeur creeps into it. It drags itself out of the dark abysm of pish, and crawls insanely up to the topmost pinnacle of tosh. It is rumble and bumble. It is flap and doodle. It is balder and dash.

He would have been merciless had he been able to lay into Obama and his speeches:

Here is a man whom we foolishly elected President, but whose speeches are devilishly calculated to disarm the sentient among us by putting them to sleep so their klepto-liberal seat-mates may more easily pick their pockets, and, once he has ceased speaking, to cause the mesmerized congregation to yell Hallelujah and begin singing hymns of evangelical if discordant praise. From a distance, and even at arm's length, one can see that the man obviously lacks some important mental faculty, mainly the capacity to remember what he intends to say.

This is a fault usually associated with the hopelessly inebriated or octogenarians trying to recall their first roll in the hay. He lacks the skill exhibited by a rural carnival barker, or by an itinerant purveyor of patent medicine. He does not trust himself to memorize any of his banal blather, which he does not write, for I do not believe for a moment that he can compose anything so simple as one of the Ten Commandments or instructions on how to open a cereal box.

He speaks without apparent notes, as many of our great orators of the past did – Patrick Henry, Calhoun, Clay – however, he performs with the aid of a toy, a fancified flash card thing usually employed by ambitious kindergarten teachers to instruct their less-than-swift charges who cannot get a point if it is buried in a six-word sentence. Moreover, Mr. Obama has two of these cheaters, one on either side of him, and perhaps a third in the middle, so that he can read them alternately and create the impression that he is including all sides of a spellbound audience as he assaults it with fresh sumptuary poppycock, when in fact he is only addressing one or the other flash card. Nevertheless, his regular Sermons on the Dais command the stupefied adoration of countless select souls eager to be saved by him. He is credibly convincing in that role, but I think the country would be at better ease if Mr. deMille lured him from the White House with a fabulous salary and cast him as a fire-breathing prophet in one of his biblical epics.

Mencken also noted (and this is Mencken, not me):

It is the invariable habit of bureaucracies, at all times and everywhere, to assume...that every citizen is a criminal. Their one apparent purpose, pursued with a relentless and furious diligence, is to convert the assumption into a fact. They hunt endlessly for proofs, and, when proofs are lacking, for mere suspicions. The moment they become aware of a definite citizen, John Doe, seeking what is his right under the law, they begin searching feverishly for an excuse for withholding it from him.

But there is one essay of his that I have wanted to tackle and rebut, which is his 1922 essay, "The Nature of Liberty," which appeared in *Prejudices* (Alfred A. Knopf, 1922). On the surface, it contradicts what he wrote about the exercise of arbitrary government power to abridge the freedom of the individual. Mencken could be said to be the grandfather of modern conservatism, a conservatism, however, not rooted in religion, not even in "tradition," but in "common sense."

In his essay, he sets up an absurd straw man, in which a non-criminal individual going home from work is accosted by a policeman who abruptly remembers a crime committed years before in another city, and accuses the citizen of the crime. The accosted citizen panics and flees, is shot by the policeman, who then uses his rosewood to beat the man senseless for resisting arrest.

Mencken wrote this in the early years of Prohibition, which he vigorously opposed, and whose deleterious economic and criminal consequences had not yet gathered steam or been realized by the time it was repealed. On the one hand, Mencken roasted Prohibition, its advocates and defenders, and its ax-wielding, Tommy gun- and billy-club-toting cops. On the other hand, he upheld the "right" of a cop to arrest a person on the most specious suspicion.

> Policemen are not given night-sticks for ornament. They are given them for the purpose of cracking the skulls of the recalcitrant plain people, Democrats and Republicans alike. When they execute that high duty they are palpably within their rights.

No mincing of meanings there. Nor here. A policeman, he writes,

> …is protected by the legislative and judicial arms in the peculiar rights and prerogatives that go with his high office, including especially the right to jug the laity at his will, to sweat and mug them, to subject them to the third degree, and to subdue their resistance by beating out their brains.

But, what about the Bill of Rights? What about unlawful arrest and incarceration. What of redress and restitution for an innocent man whose skull has been cracked? The Amendment he particularly objected to (without actually naming it in his essay) was the Fourth, which reads:

The right of the people to be secure in their persons, houses, papers, and effects, against unreasonable searches and seizures, shall not be violated, and no Warrants shall issue, but upon probable cause, supported by Oath or affirmation, and particularly describing the place to be searched, and the persons or things to be seized.

Mencken wrote about the Bill of Rights in his essay:

As adopted by the Fathers of the Republic, it was gross, crude, inelastic, a bit fanciful and transcendental. It specified the rights of a citizen, but it said nothing whatever about his duties.

I take issue with that characterization. In his essay he states that a cop has every right to arrest a citizen on his own cognizance. He is indemnified against personal error or ignorance or the injurious consequences suffered by his victim. But the indemnification assigns him the attribute of infallibility and dispenses with his error or ignorance. The citizen's "duty," on the other hand, is merely to submit to the cop's authority, regardless of his or his victim's knowledge or certainty, and regardless of the cost to the victim's livelihood and reputation.

His unfortunate disparagement of the Bill of Rights reveals a fundamental misunderstanding of its purpose. The purpose of the Bill of Rights is to act as an unequivocal and plainly worded check on government powers. It is neither to assign the citizen any duties or obligations, nor to define a reciprocal relationship between government and the citizen. It is strictly a "hands-off" and "no trespassing" warning to government.

Nearly midway in his essay, Mencken reveals his proto-conservative premises, which echo the cynical beatitudes of Thomas Hobbes and the Christian view that man is born in sin or is naturally a beast who must be constrained by law. In his obedience to a leviathan or a cop lies his salvation.

On the one hand, the citizen still retains the great privilege of membership in the most superb free nation ever witnessed on this earth. On the other hand, as a result of countless shrewd enactments and sagacious decisions, his natural lusts and appetites are held in laudable check, and he is thus kept in order and decorum.

It is reason and reality that constrain or limit men in their values and actions, not fiat law, not the most rational and wisest law. Men are not born sinners, nor as natural beasts, but *tabula rasa*. If they discard reason and flout reality, they will reap only misery, confusion, or death.

It is hard to reconcile Mencken's opposing and incompatible positions. He was right about innumerable political, cultural, and social matters. He was particularly voluble about arbitrary and tyrannical laws and statutes. But his contradictory positions on police powers are of the kind that can sanction, multiply and sire worse fallacies in the future. Observe today the timid, conciliatory Republican and conservative opposition to ObamaCare and other statist legislative landmarks of the current administration. In policy, faced with such a contradiction, most politicians habitually seize upon the worst part of it to advocate and implement, because the better part of it grants them no leave or power to indulge in their own "natural lusts and appetites."

Liberty is not a privilege or a blessing. It is a requirement for living. Knowing it demands of one, not *belief,* but absolute *certainty.*

September 2010

Amadeus: *A Pinnacle of Cultural Corruption*

Many wiser minds have written about the failure of statist economics, the fraud of "social parity," the scam of anthropogenic climate change, and the injustice and guaranteed poverty inherent in a policy of "spreading the wealth around a little." But, why does not the wisdom exhibited in these essays circulate as rapidly as does gossip, or hearsay, or scandal? Why is it so difficult to impart a general acceptance that the truisms burst in these essays were indeed lies, frauds, and deceptions?

These and other very old progressive balloons are being burst, or at least they are losing their buoyancy without the slightest prick of the needle. So many were floated with great ballyhoo and celebration, yet when they reach a certain altitude and nearness to the sun of rational scrutiny, they inevitably fall to earth, their fallacies escaping like helium through the expanded pores of the balloons' material. Their shapeless forms litter the landscape everywhere.

Allied with these phenomena are certain cultural "truisms," such as the intrinsic value of abstract and anti-art, or the noise and obscenity of rap "music" as legitimate modes of expression, or the semi-literacy that can be had in obtaining a degree in English in a community college. There are certain cinematic icons, also, that stand as truisms, such as Peter Shaffer's *Amadeus*. Salieri murdered Mozart, right?

From my childhood through adolescence and well into adulthood, I was moved by film to glean much of my knowledge of history. Having seen a film about some historical person or event, I would repair almost immediately to history books and biographies, to learn the truth. It was not that I doubted the truth of what a film conveyed. It was a hunger or a need for proof of the existence of heroism, of the exceptional, of the grand scale, of the larger-than-life. If a story contained an element of Romanticism in it – that is, a conflict requiring heroism – my disappointment in finding instead a contrary account or record, or a mass of banal irrelevancies, was balanced by the fact that the heroism or the significance of an event remained in the film and could not be altered. It remained an Aristotelian *ought*. It was of value in the culture and so one could have a kinship with that culture. It was important that I could see evidence of heroism in the real world as well as in the imaginary. It still is.

So, it never mattered to me, for example, that in Michael Curtiz's 1936 *The Charge of the Light Brigade*, the Indian Mutiny and the Crimean War were transposed in time, or that George Stevens's 1939 *Gunga Din* was a very liberal adaptation of Kipling's poem. I could cite dozens of instances.

Little did I realize that the benign fiddling with historical facts and literary works was but an innocent overture to the conscious and deliberate abandonment or disparagement of facts, and to the use of past literary and artistic accomplishments to denigrate those very facts and accomplishments in pursuit of a nihilistic agenda. As good-intentioned as they may have been in another era, these little white lies in the following era sanctioned the wholesale commission of big black ones.

As the years passed, the more "realistic" this genre of film became, the less it had to do with fact or even a suggestion of truth. At the same time, heroic spectacles largely devolved into spectacles without heroism (such as HBO's TV miniseries, *John Adams*). I noticed how carefully the new generation of movie makers attended to historical minutiæ, regardless of the period – such as clothing styles, etiquette, manners, modes of transportation, and so on – while abandoning, betraying, or omitting the truth. The "realism" hid lies, falsities, fabrications, and literary gerrymandering to accommodate political prejudices and multiculturalism. The kinship I had with the culture waned, grew cold, and finally expired. It grew into revulsion and an intolerance for what was passing for "art."

I grew to distrust the depiction in film of the life of any historical person and most adaptations of literary works. After all, I reasoned, if one is dramatizing the life of Beethoven, Edison, Patton, or even of Stalin, one must invent actions and dialogue and ascribe them to the subject. This is true even if one's purpose is benign and one does not intend to demean or whitewash the character of the subject. To present a just depiction of the subject one would need a transcript of every word and action of the person. No such record could exist or even be communicated. All one can rely on are the recorded highlights of a person's life and trusted biographies and strive for something consistent with the record or reputation. Such depictions can be illuminating if a writer or director is able to discern a person's fundamental character and possesses the skill to dramatize it. One of the best practitioners of this art was Terence Rattigan, whose dramas about T.E. Lawrence, Alexander the Great, and Lord Nelson are nonpareil delvings into the make-up of exceptional men.

But otherwise, exercising one's literary imagination in the dramatizations of especially the lives and careers of actual historic persons necessarily involves making things up and is fraught with the risk of error and subjectivism. Literary imagination is more properly applied to Aristotle's *ought*, and not to his *is*.

Aristotle, in *The Poetics*, noted: "This is why poetry [or fiction] is more philosophical than, and is superior to, history – for poetry tends to speak of universals, but history particulars." Or, as novelist-philosopher Ayn Rand, put it, in discussing Romanticism in art: "Romanticism is the *conceptual* school of art. It deals, not with the random trivia of the day, but with the timeless, fundamental, universal problems and *values* of human existence. It does not record or photograph; it creates and projects. It is concerned—in the words of Aristotle—not with things as they are, but with things as they might be and ought to be."*

"Everything you've heard is true," ends the narrator of the trailer for *Amadeus*. Well, not everything. In fact, not much is. I recall hearing the same thing said about *Bonnie & Clyde*, and any number of other "realist" films. In *Amadeus*, Shaffer neither recorded nor photographed the "particulars" of recorded history, but made things up to conform to the bile that constitutes his philosophical premises.

I make an example of *Amadeus* here because, of all the literary and esthetic felonies and larcenies committed by politically-motivated mediocrities in the 20th century in the name of "realism," *Amadeus* is by any measure one of the pinnacles of cultural corruption. This particular corruption was consciously instigated, propagated, and legitimized. It is a literary crime. The purpose of this essay is to bring some justice to the subjects of the abomination. It is by no means exhaustive; I may someday turn it into a longer, deeper study in which *Amadeus* will be but one of many instances. I am no steadfast fan of opera; I can enjoy some parts of it. This essay will focus on the biographical aspects of the composers' lives and not the esthetic merits of their work.

One need not be a musicologist, or an authority on 18th century music to argue that *Amadeus* is not a true retelling of the Mozart-Salieri rivalry, because even a cursory investigation of the lives of the two men and their careers would reveal that no such rivalry existed. Peter Shaffer's play** and film (for which he wrote the screenplay) are fraudulent, untruthful, a disgrace, and an injustice to both men. The truth about Mozart and Salieri was as readily available in the pre-Internet period of 1979 and 1984, when the play and film debuted respectively, as it is now. There was no excuse for the studied literary libel of both composers. The enormity of the lie cannot be excused by "artistic license."

From a literary standpoint, the problem with dramatizing a historical person or event is that one is limited by fact; one is not in control of what actually happened or what a person actually said or did. So one is faced with a decision: does one exaggerate or fabricate something about the person, or abandon the project? Of course, if the playwright or screenwriter adhered to the record, he would find one of two things: nothing to "dramatize" or to develop; or actions and/or characters whose dramatization is possible but which will be governed by his philosophical premises, the nature of his esthetics, and by his political leanings.

In the critical raves about *Amadeus*, the story is described as "highly fictionalized" and "loosely based." Shaffer could very well plead "artistic license" when he wrote the play and screenplay. In no way could he have "fictionalized" the alleged rivalry between the two composers, no way he could take license with what was not there.

Here is a list of all of the principal characters in *Amadeus*, and brief notations on their actual, historical roles:

Antonio Salieri (1750-1825), like his compatriot and librettist, da Ponte, was born in Venice. *Amadeus* has been responsible for the resurrection of his reputation as a prolific and more than competent composer of the 18th century. Several biographies of him were inspired as rebuttals to Shaffer's malign portrayal of him in his play and film, and his works have seen a revival. The lie became a vehicle of justice. Salieri was married in 1774, as well, and fathered eight children, hardly proof of a vow of "chastity" to God in exchange for musical talent to become as famous as Mozart.

Count Franz Xavier Wolfgang von Orsini-Rosenberg (1723-1796), the unofficial director of Hapsburg Emperor Joseph II's operas, was an early champion of Mozart, and did not try to block Mozart's appointments in the court or censor his work. He was also a career diplomat. In the film, among other actions he takes, he tears the score of the "ballet" from the sheet music of *Figaro* during a rehearsal because ballet had been banned by Joseph II. That much was true. Lorenzo da Ponte, Mozart's librettist, persuaded Joseph to attend the dress rehearsal. Seeing the dancers performing without music, Joseph asked why, and da Ponte explained. Joseph ordered the music restored. So, the conflict was not fundamentally between Rosenberg and Mozart (with Salieri managing it in the background), but between Rosenberg and da Ponte. Other than that episode, Rosenberg was not a mortal enemy of Mozart.

Count Johann Kilian von Strack (no biographical information extant) was a "groom of the chamberlain," or chamberlain of Joseph II. In short, the emperor's personal valet. ".... Strack, we are told, was an unofficial but indispensable participant in the daily music sessions as well." There is evidence that he was a cellist. In the film, he is shown as a toady and hostile to Mozart. Strack's actual attitude towards Mozart is unknown.

Baron Gottfried van Swieten (1733-1803) throughout the film is depicted as an admirer of Mozart, upbraiding him only once for his choice of Pierre Beaumarchais's *The Marriage of Figaro* as the subject of a new opera, and expressing shock at a vulgarism spoken by Mozart in the presence of the emperor. In reality, van Swieten, a diplomat and librarian, was a true friend and patron of Mozart, and there is no evidence that he questioned Mozart's taste in literature. In the play, Swieten condemns Mozart for revealing and mocking Masonic rituals in *The Magic Flute*.

Kappelmeister Giuseppe Bonno (1711-1788), in the film, the aged, rotund Italian figure who had difficulty expressing himself, was in fact a friend of the Mozart family, no stranger to Mozart's abilities, and had been in the imperial court for decades, having composed operas and oratorios. It is presumed that Bonno could speak fluent German. When he died in 1788, Salieri was appointed Kappelmeister to replace him.

The portrayal of **Count Hieronymus Joseph Franz de Paula Graf Colloredo von Wallsee und Melz**, or the **Prince-Archbishop of Salzburg** (1732-1812), was roughly consistent with the record. He regarded talented musicians appended to his court as mere servants. He disliked Mozart's independence and ultimately dismissed him, an action Mozart welcomed.

Katerina Cavalieri (1755-1801), an opera singer, is portrayed as a pupil of Salileri's who somehow contrives to play the lead role of Constanze in Mozart's *Abduction from the Seraglio*. She sang in a number of Mozart's and Salieri's operas. There is no evidence that she landed the role of Constanze in *Abduction* by sleeping with Mozart, a conclusion of Shaffer's Salieri, though there is strong evidence that she was Salieri's mistress.

The portrayal of **Leopold Mozart** (1719-1787), Wolfgang's father, in the film is barely consistent with the record – he was a "control freak" of his son and his career – although no explanation is given why. He does not appear in the play version of *Amadeus*, and was written into the film version to lend credibility to Shaffer's linkage between *Don Giovanni*, Mozart's illness, and Salieri's ruse to drive him to death by secretly commissioning the *Requiem Mass* in the evocative *persona* of Mozart's vengeful father.

Constanze Mozart (1762-1842) hardly resembled the vapid wife of Mozart in *Amadeus*. In the film she is depicted as the only daughter of Mozart's landlady, when in fact two of her older sisters were noted opera singers, while her father was a violinist. One of her sisters, Josepha, appeared as the first Queen of the Night in Mozart's *The Magic Flute*. She lived for half a century after Mozart's death in 1791, and promoted his music. She married Georg Nissen, a Danish diplomat, and arranged to have her late husband's *Requiem Mass* finished by Franz Xaver Süssmayr, an associate of Mozart's whose subsequent plan to claim the work as his own was foiled by Constanze. For an excellent recounting of the facts behind the composition of the *Requiem* and its disposition after Mozart's death, Wikipedia has a long article on the subject.

Emanuel Schikaneder (1751-1812) was a talented and ambitious impresario, composer, Shakespearean actor, and dramatist. He wrote the libretto for Mozart's *The Magic Flute* and appeared in it as Papageno. He built The Theater an der Wien, which still stands. It is not likely that Schikaneder "got physical" with Mozart, as he does in the film, for not having put *The Magic Flute* on paper. And while his troupe of actors and singers put on farces, it is not it likely, either, that he produced a parody or burlesque of Mozart's music, as occurs in the film. Nor is it likely that if he had, and Mozart saw it, Mozart would have approved.

Emperor Joseph II (1741-1790) of Austria (his full name and full titles would together occupy half a page) was the "musical king" of Austria, reformist, and enlightened despot. In the film he is portrayed as hesitant, slow-witted and open to influence by his toady entourage. In fact, he could not only read music, but play it as well as the next amateur, and not like unpromising novice, as he was depicted playing Salieri's "March of Welcome" to Mozart in the film. Further, the film leaves one with the impression that his chief calling was to attend operas and play favorites among Vienna's composers. His political life absorbed most of his energies, and other than a brief mention of the alleged danger of staging Mozart's *Figaro*, not much of his politics is evident in the film. And, there is no hint that he would predecease Mozart in 1790, exhausted from a failed military campaign against Turkey and resistance to his reforms.

Lorenzo da Ponte (1749-1838) wrote the librettos for three of Mozart's most famous operas and for a number of Salieri's. He was a Venetian republican, an admirer of Benjamin Franklin, and much like him in the character of his politics and virtuosity in various realms of culture and science. He fled the Venetian Inquisition and found work as a librettist in Vienna. In 1805, he emigrated from Britain to the United States where he lived a successful and productive life. This remarkable man is not mentioned once in either Shaffer's play or the film.

Count Franz von Walsegg (1763-1827) does not appear, either, as a character in *Amadeus*. He was, however, an amateur musician and the actual mysterious commissioner of Mozart's *Requiem Mass*. There is evidence that, once the *Requiem* was finished, he, too, intended to pass it off as his own in honor of his late wife. It appears that this was a regular habit of Walsegg's. Theft from composers was a common practice in that period. So, it was not Salieri who planned to work Mozart to death composing the *Requiem*. Shaffer, at the end of the play, through Salieri alludes to the "mysterious" commission to compose it, but does not name Walsegg.

Wolfgang Amadeus Mozart (1756-1791) has been the subject of dozens of biographies and articles. It would be fruitless to cite any one of them for they are of varying merits (and demerits). The biography I relied on most, aside from the vast sources of information on the Internet, was Piero Melograni's *Wolfgang Amadeus Mozart: A Biography*, translated by Lydia G. Cochrane (University of Chicago Press, 2007).

What was the purpose of mounting such an enormous and complicated lie about historical personages, except to destroy the good?

I can speculate only to a certain point about what moved Shaffer to choose to write about Mozart and Salieri. The subject of their alleged rivalry and poisoning was not original. Alexander Pushkin in 1830 wrote a verse story about it. Another Russian, composer Nikolai Rimsky-Korsakov, expanded the story into a one-act play in 1898. As with his imaginary Salieri, Shaffer had no imagination, no genius or creativity, and settled for an apocryphal old wives' tale to spread an untruth about two genuine creators. It is elevating gossip to the level of historical fact. This is a sign of artistic bankruptcy. But what is worse is a culture that would sanction and reward it. Shaffer simply expanded on Rimsky-Korsakov's libretto and dialogue. He was a third-hander in the transmutation of back-fence gossip into a grand-scale fraud.

The scam was extremely successful. Today, "everybody knows" that Salieri envied Mozart for his creative genius, and planned and carried out Mozart's early death. No one disputes the "fact." What was the purpose of misrepresenting Mozart and Salieri? Surely, neither Shaffer, nor Milos Forman, nor Warner Brothers would have lavished so much in the way of time, sets, cast and expense to perpetrate a lie. So, it *must* be true.

In *Honors Due*, a detective novel in which Chess Hanrahan investigates the murder of one of his favorite historians, J. Forbes Munro, and why his name paradoxically appears in the credits of a film farce about Galileo, whom the historian revered, he encounters the man's philosophy of history and biography:

> *"…Mine is not a unique approach to writing history and communicating its value. It is, frankly, traditional, but traditional only because I believe it is the single proper and profitable approach. It is at sharp odds with current approaches which, generally, seek to present historical persons and events as either nuggets of predestination or snapshots of some school's dialectical process. The modern approach denies man one of his most unique assets – indeed, his sole defining and distinguishing asset – his volition. And it denies us our critical judgment and even our purpose; it robs an individual of all recognition, of credit, of discredit, of moral approbation, as the case may be. It reduces both subject and historian to the level of programmed ants.*

> *"Galileo was not fated to write* The Starry Messenger*; nor was Cardinal Bellarmine fated to straddle an ecclesiastical fence. Napoleon need not have decided to escape from Elba; and Gordon need not have elected to remain in Khartoum. Whatever the reasons and reasoning behind it, there is no single major or minor historical event that cannot be ascribed to a conscious decision by an individual. An event, after all, is simply an action…The school that would elevate a single individual as an iconic chalice brimming with mysterious forces, and the school that would reduce him to a nearly insensate drone of a myriad of exocausative urgings, are but two sides of the same coin. I reject both."*

Amadeus is an example of the first school of history disputed by Munro. It elevated Mozart into an "iconic chalice brimming with mysterious forces," namely the ability to write great music, a phenomenon that drives the Shaffer Salieri mad because he cannot understand it.

In order to destroy the good, it was necessary to introduce a paradox. It would have been difficult for Shaffer to portray Mozart as a genius with no important, exploitable "flaws" and have Salieri envy him to the point when he would plot Mozart's murder. That would have required that Shaffer portray Salieri as a true villain, contemptible and repulsive to the core. But moral judgments are the bane of ethical relativists. So Mozart had to be portrayed as a fluke, a paradoxical contradiction, and as such earn Salieri's sanctionable and comprehensible envy and hatred. We are supposed to forgive Salieri because he could not understand why God "blessed" the buffoonish, obnoxious, filthy, vulgar, dissipated Mozart – who somehow has the ability to write "divine" music – but denied that ability to the chaste, mediocre Salieri, who was "implanted" with the desire to honor God with great music, but could never match Mozart's music. In the film, Salieri winds up blaming and hating God, as well.

The purpose was to present a contradiction that could not be resolved except by reference to the unknown and the unknowable, God and God's whimsical will: Mozart, the brilliant, creative artist who wrote glorious music, but who is portrayed as a self-absorbed narcissist, a boasting bore concerned with what others think of his work – in other words, a completely shallow vessel of nothing – and God's joke on Salieri, and, by implication, on the world.

Salieri, on the other hand, is portrayed as a wronged man moved to vengeance not only on Mozart, but on the God who allegedly blessed Mozart with an ability He denied Salieri. As a consequence, we are supposed to sympathize, if not empathize, with Salieri.

The final consensus, then, that is communicated is that both men were contemptible, perhaps even laughably so, leaving the paradox of the source of great music unknowable and unresolved. This non-resolution satisfies only two categories of minds: those who hate greatness, who say, "What's the big deal about it? It's a gift no one else has, why credit anyone with it, he didn't develop the skill, it was given to him" – and those who don't hate greatness but who wish to apologize for it and grovel before a paradox. One of those motives was Shaffer's.

Only one example of Salieri's work is shown in the film, the finale of *Axur, re d'Ormus*, which follows after excerpts from Mozart's *Figaro*. A short excerpt of an aria from it is shown in the beginning when Salieri is reminiscing about his career. This was his Italian rendition of his successful Paris opera, *Tarare*. Lorenzo da Ponte wrote the librettos for *Axur* and other of Salieri's works, as well as for Mozart's most famous operas. The longer excerpt of *Axur* in the film demonstrates that the genuine Salieri was certainly capable of composing glorious if not divinely inspired music.

Among the plot anomalies in the film, much is made of Mozart using ballet in *Figaro* in violation of Joseph II's ban of ballet in his operas. Yet, in the excerpt of the finale of *Abduction from the Seraglio*, which precedes the excerpt of *Figaro*, there is a vigorous, extended dance or ballet of dervishes and couples, choreographed by Twyla Tharp, and in a modern style I do not think was imaginable in Mozart's time. Yet, in the film, no objection is made to it by Rosenberg or by anyone else.

And in all the film, there is only one potential, dramatic conflict: When Mozart and the Emperor meet onstage after the finale of *Abduction*, Joseph remarks that there "are too many notes. Just cut a few, and it'll be perfect." Mozart, at first eager for the Emperor's approval, answers petulantly, "Which few did you have in mind, Majesty?" (The question is not asked in the play version.) Shaffer saved himself the bother of a conflict by resorting to a *deus ex machina* in the form of his future mother-in-law and her pratfall.

If there was a rivalry, it was not a bitter, personal one. It was professional one whose resolution depended on the decisions of Joseph II. But the silliness and vulgarity of Mozart could not be omitted from either the play (which underwent six versions or revisions, including the film version); that silliness and vulgarity (and the whole paradox) were absolutely necessary to Shaffer. Reading some of Mozart's correspondence, even his close-to-death correspondence, and this was hardly a man who lent himself to silliness and vulgarity in his mature years. Shaffer had to have known this.

Another author, in an earlier period, might have made something of Mozart's sanity. But, according to Shaffer's metaphysics and esthetics, there is nothing "dramatic" in sanity. So he had to make Mozart a sphinx, in Salieri's mind and in the minds of Shaffer's audiences.

I think he consciously chose to demean Mozart and Salieri. All of his plays are malevolent. The one he is most famous for after *Amadeus* is *Equus*, also made into a film. I remember thinking, when I lived in NYC and it opened on Broadway there, why would anyone want to write a whole play around a disturbed person who blinded a stable of prize horses? Most of his plays have a nihilist theme, saying more or less that without religion, man is a beast, and his "instincts" struggle against the necessity of religion.

In the film, but not in the play, probably the most benevolent character was Baron Swieten (the character with the long black hair). But in the play, he turns against Mozart because he claims Mozart revealed the Masons' "secret" rituals in *The Magic Flute* and mocked the Freemasons. But in both the play and the movie, his opposition to Mozart's choice of subject in *Figaro* is interesting. When Mozart protests, "How can we go on forever with these gods and heroes?" Swieten answers in both versions,

"Because they go on forever. They represent the eternal in us. Opera is here to ennoble us, you and me just as well as the Emperor. It is an aggrandizing art! It celebrates the eternal in Man and ignores the ephemeral. The goddess in Women and not the laundress."

But, one could take Swieten's answer and position as championing Romantic art and literature (or what passed for it in that period, the Classicist school), and Shaffer choosing to reject it, because, in his eyes, man is a beast and his pursuit of the "noble" and "eternal" is a pretense. In his metaphysics, Mozart the vulgarian is the norm, regardless of the period or era. His only salvation is to accept the will of God, come what may, and to not protest that man is corruptible and mean and small. His only salvation lies in selflessness and sacrifice. Mozart was obnoxiously selfish and greedy. And so in *Amadeus*, Salieri's fighting God's inexplicable and arbitrary will can only lead to his madness. The sole comprehensible thing is "mediocrity." The "divine" is beyond man's comprehension, and when it occurs in life, such as in a miracle, or exhibits itself in a person like Mozart, it cannot be understood.

I do not think Shaffer is just a "victim" of his education. His literary track record is consistently malevolent. A person who chooses to make a career of mocking man and commiserating in literature about man's misery and failings is not necessarily a "victim." He must feel at home in the received wisdom he never questioned. He chose to remain in it. Moreover, he was encouraged by the culture. Shaffer has been amply rewarded by it (Oscars, Tonys, the British equivalent of them, and numerous other accolades), and, as Rand put it, when she was criticizing the second-handers who were exploiting Ian Fleming's Bond novels by turning them into farces, with piles of money.***

And in the film production, Milos Forman is a partner in the libel. He knew as well as did Shaffer what the true story could have been, but chose the old wives' tale to develop and lavish with money and talent. And, as I remarked earlier, if it were not for the old wives' tale, Shaffer probably would not have chosen to write *Amadeus*. These men are not ignorant. They knew what they were doing.

In the film's opening dialogue between Salieri and the priest, Salieri asks the priest if he knows who he is. The priest answers that it makes no difference, all men are equal in God's eyes. "Are they?" replies Salieri. That establishes the theme for the rest of the story. Salieri was saying, "Well, they aren't all equal in His eyes. He bestows ability to compose great music on some, and not on others, which is unjust. He cheated me, the virtuous man dedicated to His glory, and rewarded 'the creature' who was not dedicated to His glory. But I showed Him. I murdered Mozart. Or, at least, I drove him to his death. The devil didn't make me do it. God himself did by betraying me, mocking me. But, even then, God cheated me, by foiling my plans to be credited with the great *Requiem* that was to be played at Mozart's funeral."

And not once, in either any of the play versions or the film version, does Shaffer allow Salieri to say it was true that he murdered Mozart.

Two articles can be found online that address the propagated "truisms" of *Amadeus*. One is A. Peter Brown's "'Amadeus' and Mozart: Setting the Record Straight," originally published in The American Scholar in 1992. Brown thoroughly bursts most of the balloons that surround the myth of Mozart, Salieri, and the murder hypothesis. A second article is Albert Borowitz's "Salieri and the 'Murder' of Mozart," an essay on the Tarlton Law Library Legal Studies Forum site, published in 2006. Among the many conspiracy theories discussed by Borowitz are the 19th century cottage industry of "proving" Salieri's poisoning of Mozart and the "contract" put out by the Freemasons on a disobedient member, Mozart.

An additional treasure trove of information about Mozart's relationship with the Viennese court can be found in Dorothea Link's "Mozart's Appointment to the Viennese Court."

Amadeus is the sack into which the reputations of both Mozart and Salieri were sewn by Peter Shaffer and Milos Forman, tossed ingloriously into the common grave of the undifferentiated, and sprinkled with generous shovelfuls of the lime of Critical Theory.

Well – there it is.

---

*"Introduction to *The Fountainhead*," The Objectivist, March 1968, p. 1.
**Amadeus*, A Play by Peter Shaffer. 1979. (New York: Harper Perennial, 2001).
***"Bootleg Romanticism," in *The Romantic Manifesto*, 1965. (New York: New American Library, 1971), p. 137.

November 2010

Must We 'allow' All Lliterature?

In the wake of the Mohammad cartoon controversy, I was asked by a reader if we ought to "allow" all literature– for example, literature specifically designed to engender hatred and contempt for other cultures or beliefs.

My answer: there should not be any limits placed on literature and we should "allow" all its forms. Literature by itself is inanimate; it has no volition; it cannot act. Therefore, one cannot credibly "prosecute" it, or hold it criminally responsible for actions taken by a person who has read it and might commit a crime. It is the person who is motivated by the literature who should be held responsible; after all, he chose to take the action. I stress here the role of action, or the initiation of force in a criminal act. Hate literature, such as literature that promulgates the notion of racial supremacy, bigotry, or that even advocates the overthrow of a legitimate government, cannot itself commit harm. To think it does or that it is in any way culpable is a ludicrously irrational notion that recalls the practice in the medieval era of judges trying and executing animals for crimes. It is the person or persons who take actions to advance an irrational cause who should be charged with a crime. And, here I stress crime.

Now, the authorities can be alerted to a group that distributes hate literature, and even monitor its members. But the authorities cannot legitimately act until that group takes a criminal action, such as blowing up a building, or until they have reason to believe that the group is conspiring to take such an action. And when the action is taken, then qua initiation of force, it should be deemed murder, or assault, or destruction of property, and the criminals, if apprehended, should be charged with that crime alone, and not with a "hate crime."

The concept of "hate crimes" is an insidious concession to the collectivist notion that groups have rights. Only individuals have rights. If a "hate monger" murders one individual, then the appropriate charge of murder should be laid against him. If he has committed mass murder (such as the Oklahoma City bombing), then he should be charged with as many deaths and injuries as his action caused. And with nothing more. The man who recently slashed and shot men in a Massachusetts gay bar was to be charged with a "hate crime," not just with assault with intent to kill. (He fled, and was killed in a gun battle with Arkansas police.) "Hate crime" laws are becoming a norm in the U.S., and usually carry heavier penalties than do capital crimes. Not good news.

During a trial, or during a journalistic expose of it, the hate literature that played a role in a crime can be used only to explain a motive, and of course can earn public opprobrium. (And it cannot be denied that much "hate" literature, such as the literature that claims the Holocaust never happened, is despicable.) That should be the limit of its role in the prosecution of a criminal offender. When Nazi leaders were put on trial at Nuremberg, they were not tried for the "hate" literature they were responsible for, but for their crimes of mass murder. One could claim that Hitler's Mein Kampf is hate literature and ought to be banned, or that Uncle Tom's Cabin perpetuates racial stereotypes and ought to be banned from schools and libraries. But Mein Kampf did not bring Hitler and the Nazis to power. It was a culture that put them in power, a culture that was receptive to such literature. And Uncle Tom's Cabin did not perpetuate racial stereotyping; people perpetuated their own ignorance.

In the context of the Danish cartoons and the Muslim demonstrations against them – demonstrations that in the Arab world resulted in death and destruction – it is becoming evident that the malicious signs one saw being carried in London were the work of so-called "extremists" acting on orders from Arab governments. This is just now coming out, that Muslim clerics wanted to make the cartoons an issue to test the alleged inviolacy of the freedom of speech and the West's commitment to that inviolacy. Islam is at war with the West. These "extremists" are agents of hostile foreign powers, and should be rounded up and tried as enemy agents. And if they are British citizens, they should be charged with treason and sentenced as harshly as the British allow. In either case, their placards were tantamount to a declaration of war on Britain and the West – qua their roles as agents of foreign powers.

This ought to be the policy of the United States, as well. Unfortunately, the harshest official response to the London demonstrations has been a call to adopt "hate crime" legislation (the "incitement to violence and/or murder bill"), which happens to be a subject of debate in the British parliament.

Parenthetically, in order to be clear on this point of "allowing" hate or any other kind of literature, and because my reader introduced the term "allow," the "allowance" should not be a matter of legislative permission. It is not a government's function to prescribe what is "good" literature and what is "bad," it is not its proper function to be the arbiter of the quality or content of any kind of literature, whether it is personal letters, essays, books, posters, cartoons, or propaganda, and have the power to "allow" it or prohibit it. This includes the distinctions between portraits of nudes and pornography.

The whole campaign against "hate" literature and to make its creation and propagation a capital offense is a collectivist burglary tool employed to disguise censorship by degrees. After all, who is to determine what is "hate" literature? And what could constitute it? My essays? My novels? I could write a brilliant essay against second-handers, or Islam, or southern Baptists, or homosexuality. I'm sure someone who reads it might deem it "hate" literature. He is free to disagree with it, and to call it what he wishes, but not free to physically assault me or imprison me or ask the government to punish me because his "sensibilities" have been "offended," or in any way to deprive me of my liberty and freedom to write. He can always walk away from it, or ignore it, or compose a rebuttal.

In the same way, Muslims can ignore cartoons of Mohammed. Those who don't reveal their real agenda: they want to subvert the concept of freedom of speech in order to shield themselves from legitimate criticism and opprobrium. It is not irrational skinheads or racists they want protection from, but rather rational, reasoning individuals whom they could not rebut in civilized discourse. You might have noticed in the news that some mullahs, imams and even "distinguished" Islamic scholars at universities are "deploring" the violent demonstrations, chiefly because they claim the protests are giving Islam a "bad name." Too late, that! They are merely playing "good cop, bad cop" with the West, and their protestations are just more yadda-yadda-yadda lip service to beguile the unwary and disarm the undiscriminating.

One Islamic scholar from the American University in Washington this morning on ABC complained in an interview with Charley Gibson that the violence is damaging the move to reconcile the irreconcilable between Islam and the West. Jesus Christ and Jews, however, are legitimate subjects of virulent Arab cartoons; prophets are not. He asserted that it is incumbent upon Westerners to understand this and extend the hand of tolerance and respect, while rank and file Muslims don't need to understand us. He might have added: We are just the infidels ready for beheading and slaughter unless we submit and become servile, ingenuous followers.

Gibson brought up the subject of Jill Carroll, the kidnapped reporter facing execution, and the murders by Islamic "extremists" of Westerners and even other Muslims, but the scholar danced around that and left Gibson sounding like Elmer Fudd. Gibson, like many Western journalists, just couldn't grasp the either/or ultimatum lurking in the scholar's gentle, seductively unbombastic rhetoric.

The only literature that can be held responsible for a consequence is libel – that is, the author of a libel can be held responsible – when someone's written or broadcast words demonstrably damage a person's livelihood or reputation. Slander is a form of libel. These actions, however, are not crimes, but civil torts to be adjudicated in a civil, not a criminal, court.

I might add that the Danish cartoons are not instances of slander or libel. Nor can they be called "hate speech" or "hate literature." Islam, like Christianity, Hinduism, or any other system of mysticism, is just that:

mysticism posing as a moral code based on the unprovable existence of a commandment-issuing ghost. Any organized faith or creed is a legitimate target for mockery or satire because it is the epitome of irrationality and foolishness. All creeds are merely elaborate systems of tarot cards, Ouija boards and crystal balls supplemented by voluminous instruction manuals, and we do not scruple to satirize those frauds and their "prophets."

How often was Richard Nixon caricatured by cartoonists and in television satire as an oily used car salesman? Or Gerald Ford as a bumbler prone to "locomotion malfunctions"? Did those portrayals result in riots or demonstrations by used car salesmen or fiery rampages by the lame and halt? No. Nor did Nixon, Ford, the used car salesmen or the lame and halt sue for their presumably injured "sensibilities."

One can't slander or libel the irrational. One's aim is to stylistically ridicule it, to cause people to recognize and laugh at the irrational or the foolish, to not take it seriously, to communicate to them a faith's inherent appeal to dupes and fools. Islam, however, is an especial candidate for satire and mockery, since under its drab patina of daily humility, devotion and selflessness lurks a bloodthirsty, homicidal maniac. This has been demonstrated countless times; the consistent, truly devout are obeying the central tenets of the creed, and the "Arab street" follows and sanctions. Now, if one calls a killer a killer, verbally or in print, to his face or in an editorial or a cartoon, is that an instance of slander or libel? No. That is identifying a fact. And if a mystic or killer demands "respect" for his beliefs and asks us to refrain from "insulting" them, he is asking us for the unearned, for an esteem to which the irrational is not entitled.

So, all forms of literature are rationally permissible – that is, free to be written or expressed. To paraphrase a popular saying in the U.S., "Literature doesn't shoot people, people shoot people." If governments or courts begin to regulate literature, however, then that initiation of force – or censorship – would justify the only means left for a free people to save themselves from slavery or secular dhimmitude: to revolt, or, as the heroes in Rand's Atlas Shrugged did, go "on strike," which is much the same thing.

February 2006

Hollywood vs. America

"**W**hen's the movie coming out?"

I have been asked that question repeatedly over the course of seven years of book-signings for *Sparrowhawk* at Colonial Williamsburg's Booksellers by eager patrons who have read the series and wish to see it on the big screen.

"Not any time soon," I usually answer. "If it is ever produced, it won't be by Hollywood. And if Hollywood in some episode of hubris thought it could tackle it, it would attempt to maul and dismember it, just out of sheer, doctrinaire meanness, coupled with incompetence. I would likely disown the result. After all, Hollywood hates America."

I borrow the title of film critic Michael Medved's book-long critique of Hollywood (*Hollywood vs. America: Popular Culture and the War on Traditional Values* (New York: HarperCollins, 1992). Neither he nor his book is the subject here, but rather the culture that cannot produce *Sparrowhawk* or any other nominally pro-American, pro-freedom film – including the "traditional" ones which Medved has championed in his book and in various conservative and religious columns (promoting family, God, and other, non-intellectual, non-fundamental values – "Leave It to Beaver" style, with Ward Cleaver taking questions from the audience).

I don't think a list of films is necessary that proved Hollywood's anti-Americanism. I could go as far back as some of Frank Capra's films (which were not so much anti-American as pro-collectivist), and, working forward, see the list of movies grow exponentially (with a short hiccup in the 1950's and early 1960's), ending with stuff like "Avatar" or "Little Big Man" or "Jarhead."

The worst film critics happen to be conservative ones. They call for a moral cinema and constantly pine for one that does not now exist. Leftist critics have a near monopoly in the press and mainstream media, but their influence and popularity poll are hard to measure. But, as the Republicans in politics are bankrupt of ideas and cannot (or will not) offer a credible antidote to the leftist ideology of the current administration that does not include God, conservative critics like Medved cannot offer a credible antidote to the leftist mantra that America is an evil country, and an evil empire, and evil in its material comfort and achievements.

Leftists are beholden to the great ghost *society*; rightists are beholden to a ghost of indeterminate gender and appearance in the ether (or perhaps He's a resident of the constellation Orion, no theologian in history has been able to pinpoint his whereabouts on the map). The leftists have been able to put over their ghost because *society* is ostensibly tangible: it's you, and me, and our neighbors all over the country. The rightists can only cite *belief* that the creator of individual rights and freedom exists – somewhere, as an entity of semi-infinite dimensions, armed with the contradictory powers of omniscience and omnipotence – and that everything good emanates from Him, including that incidental, unimportant thing called capitalism.

In terms of metaphysics and epistemology, the leftists have a leg up on the rightists. They can "prove" their ghost exists, and why everyone should defer to it today, in personal relationships on up to coercive legislation, while all the rightists can trot out is a tooth fairy on steroids who mandates selflessness and self-sacrifice in the name of life after death.

David Brooks, writing in The New York Times, has written about "Avatar" and the Haitian earthquake. Brooks is a specter himself, materializing here as a progressive, there as a disgruntled conservative. His advice on why the Haitian earthquake was so destructive is nearly spot-on. Haiti has been the recipient of billions in especially U.S. aid to reduce its poverty, yet its infrastructure collapsed and vanished like sand castles at the onset of high tide. Haiti remains the poorest country in the Western hemisphere. Why?

The first of those truths is that we don't know how to use aid to reduce poverty. Over the past few decades, the world has spent trillions of dollars to generate growth in the developing world. The countries that have not received much aid, like China, have seen tremendous growth and tremendous poverty reductions. The countries that have received aid, like Haiti, have not.

Here he implies, but does not identify, that it is freedom that allows countries that have not received aid (extorted from productive men in freer countries) to increase the wealth and standard of living of their citizens. China, even though it is a repressive dictatorship, allows its citizens a modicum of freedom in order to produce wealth (to better tax and expropriate). Countries that receive aid become addicted to it and never develop the morality or political institutions that promote wealth-creation. They remain on welfare, and are not encouraged to break free of it by the "humanitarian" programs of the West, which has a vested interest in being altruistic, altruism being the only virtue it boasts (and which is destructively addictive in its own right). Altruism, after all, is the enemy of selfishness and self-interest. Why would a tax-paid alms-giver want to see a country like Haiti become free of his generosity?

Brooks shows the other side of his spectral being when discussing James Cameron's "Avatar." (Avatar: incarnation of Hindu deity: an incarnation of a Hindu deity in human or animal form, especially one of the incarnations of Vishnu such as Rama and Krishna.) In "The Messiah Complex," he rightly points out that the film is a 3-D rehash of cinematic shibboleths from the last few decades of Hollywood America-bashing: colonialism is bad, the white race is bad, capitalism is bad, and so they're doomed to be defeated by the primitive natives. He mocks the film better than I could.

This is the oft-repeated story about a manly young adventurer who goes into the wilderness in search of thrills and profit. But, once there, he meets the native people and finds that they are noble and spiritual and pure. And so he emerges as their Messiah, leading them on a righteous crusade against his own rotten civilization.

Avid moviegoers will remember "A Man Called Horse," which began to establish the pattern, and "At Play in the Fields of the Lord." More people will have seen "Dances With Wolves" or "The Last Samurai." Kids have been given their own pure versions of the fable, such as "Pocahontas" and "Fern Gully."

John Podhoretz in The Weekly Standard, whom Brooks cites, is even more severe:

> What they didn't tell us is that Avatar is blitheringly stupid; indeed, it's among the dumbest movies I've ever seen. Avatar is an undigested mass of clichés nearly three hours in length taken directly from the revisionist westerns of the 1960s-the ones in which the Indians became the good guys and the Americans the bad guys. Only here the West is a planet called Pandora, the time is the 22nd century rather than the 19th, and the Indians have blue skin and tails, and are 10 feet tall.

> They're hunters and they kill animals, but after they do so, they cry and say it's sad. Which only demonstrates their superiority. Plus they have (I'm not kidding) fiber-optic cables coming out of their patooties that allow them to plug into animals and control them. Now, that just seems wrong-I mean, why should they get to control the pterodactyls? Why don't the pterodactyls control them? This kind of biped-centrism is just another form of imperialist racism, in my opinion.

(I especially appreciated Podhoretz's remark about the natives apologizing to the animals they kill. That politically-correct and probably fictive Indian practice was in the opening scene of the last remake of "Last of the Mohicans" (1992), another turned-inside-out mess which partly moved me to begin work on *Sparrowhawk*.)

Podhoretz writes, observing the anti-Americanism in the movie:

You're going to hear a lot over the next couple of weeks about the movie's politics-about how it's a Green epic about despoiling the environment, and an attack on the war in Iraq, and so on. The conclusion does ask the audience to root for the defeat of American soldiers at the hands of an insurgency. So it is a deep expression of anti-Americanism-kind of.

But while Brooks and Podhoretz justly explode the story and dwell on the suffocating political correctness and second-handedness of "Avatar," they don't defend or advocate anything. Neither of them contends that our civilization is not rotten, that it ought to be defended and preserved, and that it is superior to Pandora's and even Haiti's. Neither counters the charge that big corporations are inherently evil, and that its employees are necessarily avaricious monsters capable only of destruction.

Most conservatives are too cowed by their own apologetic philosophy to advocate the superiority of Western culture over Islamic or any other pre-industrial or anti-reason culture. They would be reluctant to take Voodooism to task, for fear of offending a cultural "tradition." When was the last time Britons heard that British culture was superior to that of the Muslims who want to establish Britain as a suburb of Riyadh? And where, except on Internet blogs, do Americans read that their civilization is superior to the Indians'? It is such 'sensitivity" to Muslim culture that freed Major Nidal Hasan to open up on American soldiers at Fort Hood, in the same way that "sensitivity" to Pandoran culture freed neo-Na'vi Jake Sully to open up on his fellow humans in "Avatar."

It is this crucial omission (or evasion) by conservatives which allows them to agree with their rivals for political power, the leftists. As the leftists cannot bring themselves to champion individual rights, private property, and selfishness, neither can the rightists. They meet on a middle ground, as they have done for decades in Congress, and agree to an alleged compromise that simply paves the way for the more consistent of them to go whole-hog. As the Obama administration has done.

The Republicans are as anti-American as are the Democrats. As is Hollywood. The film that defines America is neither "Wall Street" nor "The Ten Commandments," but, to date, "The Fountainhead."

December 2010

Enshrining Sacrifice: The American Film Institute's 'inspiring' Film List

It was inevitable, almost predestined, that Frank Capra's cinematic paean to selflessness and self-sacrifice, "It's a Wonderful Life" (1946), would be voted the most inspiring American film out of one hundred candidates by the American Film Institute. In a culture that values altruism as a primary, uncontroversial, not-to-be-questioned virtue, it is almost an instance of determinism.

On its official website, the AFI's director and CEO, Jean Picker Firstenberg, explained the purpose of the program that aired the choices on national television on June 14:

"The past few years have not been easy in America – from September 11th to the devastation of hurricanes Katrina, Rita and Wilma. AFI's 100 years....100 Cheers will celebrate the films that inspire us, encourage us to make a difference and send us from the theatre with a greater sense of possibility and hope for the future."

The website notes: "AFI distributed a ballot in November 2005 with 300 nominated inspiring movies to a jury of over 1,500 leaders from the creative community, including film artists (directors, screenwriters, actors, editors, cinematographers), critics and historians."

"To make a difference," in the context of the Capra film, is a euphemism for selfless efforts on behalf of others, for "giving back" to society, to the "community," to the world.

The AFI program, broadcast under the title "Cheers," elaborates on its moral criteria of the "most inspiring:

"Movies that inspire with characters of vision and conviction who face adversity and often make a personal sacrifice for the greater good. Whether these movies end happily or not, they are ultimately triumphant – both filling audiences with hope and empowering them with the spirit of human potential."

And therein is the clincher: "sacrifice for the greater good."

In previous commentary, I cited Bill Gates's decision to "give back" his billions as an auspicious instance of craven selflessness in a commitment to "make a difference for the greater good." It is his money, and he has a right to dispose of it as he wishes. One can think of a number

170

of "worthier" things he could spend the money on than on the insatiable demands of the needy, such as the endowment of a university fully staffed by advocates of reason and freedom.

However, one would like to ask him: "On the premise that you are giving back to society what you took from it, what exactly is it that you took? Ideas for software? Programming innovations? If you concede that you originated those things, and not society, why are you branding yourself as a thief or a repentant debtor? If you concede that you took your customers' money in trade, why do you believe that you don't deserve every penny of it? Haven't your products revolutionized men's lives and made an incalculable difference? If you concede that you gave the public a priceless value, why are you willing to believe that it was immoral, immaterial, or irrelevant, and that you must make amends?"

But it is nearly futile to argue with a convert to altruism. One's only weapon is reason. Altruism is reason-proof. It derogates the self and selfishness. It is a corrosive that eats away at a mind and renders it progressively impervious to rational persuasion. It is why I rarely attempt to persuade an otherwise rational person of the folly and impracticality of his altruist beliefs. To make the transition from an altruist morality to one of rational selfishness requires too great a mental task for a person who at least senses the rightness of a refutation of altruism; he would see that he would need to repudiate nearly everything on which he has based his life. It is too frightening or traumatic a prospect, and the person will choose instead to "blank out" without pursuing the subject privately or in conversation.

This is not so much a digression as it is an elucidation. To the AFI, the term "inspiration," in a literary or artistic context, refers almost exclusively to the motivation to practice altruism and self-sacrifice. It has nothing to do with what Ayn Rand called "spiritual fuel" to pursue or fight for one's values. In her essay, "What is Romanticism?" in The Romantic Manifesto, she writes:

> "The archenemy and destroyer of Romanticism was the altruist morality. Since Romanticism's essential characteristic is the projection of values, particularly moral values, altruism introduced an insolvable conflict into Romantic literature from the start. The altruist morality cannot be practiced (except in the form of self-destruction) and, therefore, cannot be projected or dramatized convincingly in terms of man's life on earth...."

In that same essay, she notes:

"Romanticism is a category of art based on the recognition of the principle that man possesses the faculty of volition.....If man possesses volition, then the crucial aspect of his life is his choice of values – if he chooses values, then he must act to gain and/or keep them – if so, then he must set his goals and engage in purposeful action to achieve them."

Some of the films that made the top 100 list are "inspiring" for the right reasons, that is, they do not inspire one to devote one's life to others' needs or to sacrifice anything, but dramatize the pursuit of personal values. The values they dramatize the pursuit of are as varied as the subjects and themes of the films. And some of them dramatize apparent sacrifices which are actually actions taken at risk to preserve values.

To cite an example from the AFI list, "Gunga Din" is about a water-carrier for the British army in India. He wants to be a regular soldier in that army, but is scoffed for his ambition. He risks his life to warn the army of a trap, and is killed. This is not so much a "sacrifice" as his achieving his goal of being a soldier (and his knowing the risks of being one). The same could be said about "Glory," in which the principal characters die as soldiers risking their lives to fight for their values. About these and a few other films that feature the risks of warfare, the last thing one would want to hear is President Bush pontificating on the virtue of sacrifice in relation to collectivist or altruist goals. Bush and Hollywood, ostensibly enemies, have more in common than either would be willing to acknowledge.

I personally find these inspiring stories. On the other hand, as a teenager I found the deterministic, Shakespearian "Lawrence of Arabia" inspiring not only for its numerous production values (such as direction, cinematographer, casting, and dialogue), but chiefly because it suggested what is possible if those same production values were applied to Romantic stories.

The majority of the films on the AFI list, however, fall somewhere in between value-pursuit and value-sacrifice, or have little or nothing to do with either end, such as "2001: A Space Odyssey." The list is as mixed as an altruist's premises. One revolts against the presence of some films on the same list as others. "Shane" and "High Noon" should not be in the same company with "Harold and Maude" and "Dances with Wolves." It is also worth noting that "The Fountainhead" did not make it to the list.

There is no room here to discuss all one hundred films on the AFI list of the "most inspiring." That would require a book. But an Associated Press article on the AFI list is instructive about the moral esteem in which "It's a Wonderful Life" is held in modern culture. It is the story of George Bailey, who surrenders his personal ambition to the needs of his "community," is about to commit suicide, when, as the A.P. article describes it, he "got a chance to see how ugly the world would be without him" had he not been born, that is, conned into relinquishing that ambition. At movie's end, George's brother, referring to all the people in Bedford Falls George has "helped," proclaims him the richest man in the town.

"We all connect to that story," said Bob Gazzale, producer of the AFI TV special. "We may not all connect to the story of a fighter from Philadelphia or a singing family in the Austrian Alps. But there's no way to get away from the inspiring story of George Bailey. It relates to us all."

No, it does not, if by "relate" he means that we all have the potential for selflessness or self-sacrifice, or the capacity to tolerate it for the sake of others' needs, as George Bailey chose to tolerate it. The first time I saw the Frank Capra film as a child, I was repelled by it, and for a long time was intrigued about why it was so revered. As a novelist, I have always wanted to rewrite that story. But Ayn Rand beat me to it in Atlas Shrugged, the story about heroes who refuse to be George Baileys.

It would be interesting to speculate on whether or not Bill Gates, now the richest man in the world, found "It's a Wonderful Life" the most inspiring movie he ever saw, and whether or not he ever privately wondered, at the peak of his career, when he was being sued by rivals and hounded by the U.S. government and the European Union, what the world would be like had he not pursued his own selfish ambition to create Microsoft, or if he now withdrew the products of his mind. That, however, would necessitate the self-esteem of a man proud of his achievements, together with a knowledge of the injustices perpetrated against him. Bill Gates lacks both that self-esteem and a sense of justice; he is motivated by humility and mercy, the twin enemies of justice. He meets the criteria of a sacrificer for the "greater good."

June 2006

Obama's Malice Aforethought

President Barack Obama's feelings are hurt.

For most of his time in the White House, Obama has been critical of information about him and his administration posted on the Internet. He's frequently denigrated bloggers and Internet conservative news & commentary web sites for their efforts to cover stories the so-called mainstream news media refuse to cover, according to critics of his plans to control the "Information Highway."

This is precisely the kind of speech that Obama and his unelected czars and wannabe censors wish to monitor, judge, squelch, punish, crush, and eradicate. Permanently. Napoleon shared the same touchiness: "I fear the newspapers more than a hundred thousand bayonets." And those newspapers, together with the bayonet thrusts of bloggers, conservative (and non-conservative) news and commentary websites, have needled Obama and his staff and advisors beyond endurance. Any words critical of Obama or the government has been regarded as the equivalent of blasphemy, slander, libel, and the subverting the "community harmony" of the nation.

In an interview with Rolling Stone Magazine, Obama, when asked about his media nemesis Fox News, remarked:

> (Laugh) Look, as president, I swore to uphold the Constitution, and part of that Constitution is a free press. We've got a tradition in this country of a press that oftentimes is opinionated. The golden age of an objective press was a pretty narrow span of time in our history. Before that, you had folks like Hearst who used their newspapers very intentionally to promote their viewpoints. I think Fox is part of that tradition – it is part of the tradition that has a very clear, undeniable point of view. It's a point of view that I disagree with. It's a point of view that I think is ultimately destructive for the long-term growth of a country that has a vibrant middle class and is competitive in the world. But as an economic enterprise, it's been wildly successful. And I suspect that if you ask Mr. Murdoch what his number-one concern is, it's that Fox is very successful."

Obama may have sworn to uphold the Constitution, but in his realm of pragmatism, words are cheap, their meanings are negotiable. As one blogger noted about his position on the Second Amendment, "Obama's position on the 2nd Amendment has one more side than a polygon." He has done everything in his power to usurp the Constitution.

A free press – or freedom of speech – is not a "tradition," but a right founded on the nature of man and the political requirements to preserve his freedom, one of which is property. What "golden age of an objective press" was he referring to, and what would he define as an "objective press"? The mainstream media that helped get him elected?

He called Fox News "wildly successful," but what did he mean by that? As virtually the only television news outlet that has consistently criticized Obama and promoted his critics, it has been "wildly successful" in alerting the public to his and Congress's machinations. He was not paying Fox News a compliment. Fox News' freedom of speech is "ultimately destructive." Destructive of what? His socialist agenda? What has Fox News's position to do with a "vibrant middle class," "long-term growth," and being "competitive in the world"? These are non sequiturs issues picked out of the air to fill space. Behind his laughter was a suppressed growl.

Even a "temporary" or "emergency" lock-up of this kind of speech is intolerable. Under a *statist* regime, "temporary" means permanently. The regime also decrees what is an "emergency." Nazi Germany existed in a state of permanent emergency, from the day Hitler came to power in 1933 to its collapse in 1945. Obama and his allies in government are pining for a Nazi-style "Ministry of Public Enlightenment and Propaganda" that would filter, interpret, suppress, and outlaw news and information they deem harmful to and critical of the government's policies, powers, and actions.

The Obama administration, at first defensive of its powers, policies and actions, has conducted an offensive against any and all who question the motive and wisdom of that administration.

Obama's administration is definably *statist*. What is *statism*? Encarta's *World English Dictionary,* offers the best "mainstream" definition: *the theory, or its practice, that economic and political power should be controlled by a central government leaving regional government and the individual with relatively little say in political matters.*

That definition fits the Obama administration like a glove, a glove that fits neatly over the mailed fist clenched behind the back of every one of his appointees (remaining or departed).

The definition, however, omits or neglects the fundamental philosophical foundation of statism. Novelist/philosopher Ayn Rand delves beneath the obvious description to the roots:

> The political expression of altruism is collectivism or *statism,* which holds that man's life and work belong to the state—to society, to the group, the gang, the race, the nation—and that the state may dispose of him in any way it pleases for the sake of whatever it deems to be its own tribal, collective good.

And:

> Statism—in fact and in principle—is nothing more than gang rule.
> A dictatorship is a gang devoted to looting the effort of the
> productive citizens of its own country.

De facto censorship or semi-regulated speech, not overtly
controlled by the government, but ominous and damaging all the same, has
crept into the culture. Submission to the wishes of Islamic activists not to
reproduce pictures of Mohammad, or to criticize Islam at all, is a recent
example of self-censorship. It also takes the form of self-suppression and
compliance as a result of a threat from a non-governmental agency, such
as the Center for Science in the Public Interest (CSPI), which recently
"persuaded" the ice cream maker, Ben & Jerry's, to remove its description
"all natural" from its product line. (I am no fan of Ben & Jerry's, which,
before it was acquired by Unilever, was a regular donor of its profits to
virtually every left-wing and environmentalist group in the country;
compliance with the complaint was in the way of just desserts and a
consequence of its support for one of its destroyers.)

The CSPI, based in Washington, said the government should
define the term."The Food and Drug Administration could do consumers
and food manufacturers a great service by actually defining when the word
'natural' can and cannot be used to characterize a given ingredient," CSPI
Executive Director Michael F. Jacobson said in a statement.

So, the CSPI wishes the FDA to define terms. Well, let us see how
the censors and their patrons *do not* think about the phrase "all natural."
Ice cream is not "natural," that is, it is man-made and not found in
"nature." But why are man-made entities excluded from "nature" or barred
from being deemed "natural"? If it exists, it is indeed "natural," or *of*
nature, even though it is manufactured. Ice cream must be made from
things that exist and rearranged by man. So, ice cream can truly and
literally be said to be "all natural," *including* the additives and ingredients
cited by the CSPI. The phrase *all natural* is, therefore, an oxymoron.

But in this instance the term "all natural" is not being employed by
the "pure food and drug" police as a scientific term. It is used exclusively
as a political weapon and a brandished club to compel compliance with the
whims of the CSPI.

Freedom of speech is guaranteed by the First Amendment of the
U.S. Constitution. It is disliked by tyrants. It is disliked by Obama and his
cohorts in the administration and Congress Why? Because it facilitates
communication between those who practice it and those who audit it,
Because by allowing those who have an opinion or point of view to

express it to those who are receptive to it, it may lead to action that could checkmate or obviate fiat power and the ongoing violation of individual rights. Because it exposes tyrants and their lies and machinations and power-lusting ambitions. Because it is a vehicle of the truth. Because it is a source of knowledge. Because its guarantee of unregulated, uncontrolled, unsuppressed knowledge can precipitate trouble for tyrants.

It is this freedom of speech which has led to the Tea Party and to the wide dissatisfaction of Americans with Obama and Congress, and to the likely defeat of the Democrats in the coming midterm elections, a defeat virtually ensured by the authoritarian legislation passed by Congress and advocated and encouraged by Obama. The dumbing-down of Americans in public education has not been entirely successful; there are still enough Americans left who possess a sense of imperiled and outraged self and a focused concern that is reflected in the polls and in anti-government rhetoric and on numerous websites dedicated to broadcasting the truth.

One of the most recent and insidious means of *de facto* censorship is what is called "libel tourism," an action taken by a foreign national to suppress criticism of him in this country by ruinous litigation.

> The story of the SPEECH Act starts with Dr. Rachel Ehrenfeld, the director of the American Center for Democracy, who bravely stood up to a Saudi billionaire named Khalid bin Mahfouz whom she accused of financing terrorist groups in her book, *Funding Evil: How Terrorism is Financed – and How to Stop It.* Mahfouz, who died of a heart attack on August 16, 2009, targeted Ehrenfeld with a lawsuit as he had done to other authors accusing him of having ties to terrorism. Taking advantage of the United Kingdom's libel laws that force the defendant to prove their accusations in court, Mahfouz sued 45 publishers and journalists and all settled, except for Dr. Ehrenfeld.

> Following a law passed by New York State that did not recognize the jurisdiction of foreign libel laws in that state, Congress passed its own version of the law.

> On August 10, a major victory for freedom of speech was achieved. President Obama signed the Securing the Protection of our Enduring and Established Constitutional Heritage Act (SPEECH Act) into law, stopping Americans from being sued for libel by individuals in other countries with inadequate First Amendment rights. The legislation is a defeat for those who would

seek to silence Americans speaking out against radical Islam by threatening to bankrupt them with costly lawsuits.

Given Obama's "outreach" efforts to the Islamic world, together with his refusal to take anything but a Pollyannaish perspective on Islam's religious ideology, a perspective which denies its perils – one of them the brutal silencing of any and all criticism of Islam – he must have signed that law with gnashing teeth and a hurried flair of his pen. He could not very well have *not* signed it, because it passed Congress unanimously.

Glib speakers like President Barack Obama can be boring or enervating, but nevertheless dangerous. His tenure in the White House has allowed him to not only reveal his core, anti-freedom, anti-liberty, anti-American premises, but those of his allies in and out of government. They have become emboldened in their designs to establish their own satrapies of power, power that would comport with his own and answerable to him.

Proposed cybersecurity legislation circulating on Capitol Hill would give the president the power to declare an emergency in the case of big online attacks and force some businesses to beef up their cyber defenses and submit to scrutiny. The draft bill, a copy of which was obtained by Reuters, allows the president to declare an emergency if there is an imminent threat to the U.S. electrical grid or other critical infrastructure such as the water supply or financial network because of a cyber attack.

What is proposed in the bill is *de facto* nationalization of businesses deemed by the government to be "critical." This is a signature sign of fascism.

> Steve DelBianco, director of the trade group NetChoice, whose members include Yahoo, eBay and News Corp., objected to a part of the bill that would bar companies designated as "critical" from fighting that designation in court. "That has to be amended to make this bill fair to the businesses who will pay for it," he said. The draft tries to calm fears the government is reaching too far into business operations by requiring specific designations for which parts of a company or industry might be considered "critical infrastructure."

Obama's statements indicate not so superfluous a revelation as his "mindset" as a compulsive, ideological predisposition to control what is said about him and his policies and what he wishes not to be said about him and his policies. His statements about freedom of speech.

Government controlled media and speech are not free media and free speech. Government controlled news is not news but falsehoods, half-truths disguising lies, and fairy tales spun for the gullible and the ignorant.

Fortunately, if only temporarily, Obama and his gang know that the jig is up, insofar as the midterm elections are concerned. Seeing the signs of an uncompromising rejection of the administration's policies (at least by the American people, but not by the Republicans), many of his key advisors and appointees are jumping the Titanic before they are sucked into the vortex of ignominious defeat. Obama's once highly-charged public performances are now insouciant to the point of boredom. His papered halls fool no one, not even him.

Yet, he will have two more years left in his term. He is still a danger to contend with. He will try to abridge the First Amendment under the guise of the "public interest." His pronouncements on the Constitution are directly pronouncements on property rights, on which is dependent freedom of speech. As long ago as 2001, he claimed.

> But, the Supreme Court never ventured into the issues of *redistribution of wealth*, and of more basic issues such as political and economic justice in society. To that extent, as radical as I think people try to characterize the Warren Court, it wasn't that radical. It didn't break free from the essential constraints that were placed by the Founding Fathers in the Constitution....(*Italics* mine)

He was wrong about that, because the Court has often decided to redistribute wealth, but that is another issue. The key issue here is that he knows that "redistributed wealth" also means redistributed *privileges* of speech. And if one has no influence or pull in the government, then chances are one will not be allowed to speak.

A position such as he articulated in 2001 and has repeated since then constitutes malice aforethought. He knows what he is doing. Americans should be advised to say so as vigorously and often as they can.

December 2010

§   The End   §